My SOUL'S JOURNEY

My SOUL'S JOURNEY

*My struggle to understand
what I always felt to be true*

MIDGE BRAXTON

Printed in the United States of America

First Edition
Printed in 2015 in the United States of America

Book designed by Ian Berg

ISBN-13: 978-0692635513
ISBN-10: 0692635513

DEDICATION

This book is dedicated to my son,
Brodey Angelo Braxton.

It is our story

CONTENTS

ACKNOWLEDGMENTS

THERE ARE so many people who have made this book possible. To my husband Dave, without you there would not have been a story to tell. You are my best friend, my other half and my strength. To my family for always standing with me and encouraging me to keep going. To my children, you are the light in my life. To my friend Betsy Yespelkis who has always been one of my biggest cheerleaders. My editors, Mike Valentino and Erin Braxton. Last but certainly not least, to Leanne, who took me on a three hour journey one evening that would change my life.

PROLOGUE

"WOW, THERE are a lot of people here behind you. They are all so happy that you are here and there is so much love for you in this room." Leanne sits back and stops for a moment. "Ok, they are saying something about a baby. Do you have a baby?" I say only yes, because I don't want to say too much or give anything away. "They want to talk about him."

"They are all behind you, motioning to their faces," she says, adding, "his face is very different from yours. There is nothing wrong with him, he is just very different. Does this make sense?"

"Yes."

At this point Leanne sits back and closes her eyes. She then says, "This doesn't make sense to me, so I am going to say exactly what I am hearing. Please let me know if it makes sense to you, is that ok?"

I nodded and motioned for her to go on.

"They are saying that the way this child came into this world, was strictly a vessel for bringing his soul to you. Your souls were always meant to be together, his soul was meant to be with you. Does that make any sense to you?"

Ok, WOW, yes, yes, yes! Not only did it make sense to me, but right when she said that, it was like a bolt of lightning to my chest. My confirmation -- finally -- that what I had always felt to be true, actually was! "Yes, I understand what that means," I say.

She sits back again and a few seconds later she opens her eyes and says, "Oh my goodness I just heard, 'he is adopted.' Now it all makes sense."

Through the tears all I can say is, "Yes."

INTRODUCTION

HAVE YOU ever met someone for the first time and felt a connection, not just that you have met them before, but deep down in your soul, *know* you have known them before?

Have you ever been somewhere you have never been before, and had an overwhelming feeling or have been overcome with emotion *knowing* that you have been there before?

Have you ever awoken from a dream *knowing* and feeling in your heart that you have been blessed with a visit from a loved one who has passed? That they were right there with you?

Have you ever felt deep down in your soul that someone is missing in your life? That a piece of your soul is missing? Someone you may have "left behind"?

All of these things have happened in my life and there is an unbelievable happiness when you are able to recognize them. I have learned so much and have made some mistakes, but overall have been blessed beyond belief by those who have joined me on this journey that God has directed for me. This is the story of my soul through this lifetime, and its interaction with the souls with which it was meant to walk.

Xác nhận của bệnh viện

Trưởng khoa

11 / 3 / 2007

chị Anh từ

Lê Phạm

"This past weekend we told everyone in our family about adopting you. They are all so excited for us and can't wait to meet you."

Journal entry 4/15/07

FAMILY LIFE

I WAS born in a small suburban town of Philadelphia at the end of 1964, a time when our country was continuing to heal one year after the assassination of John F. Kennedy. The Beatles had invaded our shores in a big way, and Americans were just beginning to hear of a faraway place called Vietnam. Ours was a typical small town family. My parents had met at my grandparents' coffee shop, my dad was a police officer in the town and my mom worked at the shop. She would wait on him when he came in for his coffee and save him a special danish. They were married in 1962, moved into a house my dad had bought, and in the next eight years had four daughters. My poor father was so outnumbered, we even had a female dog named, what else, Girlie!

I remember the night my sister Lois was born; I was six years old. My dad woke us up in the middle of the night and took us to Nan and Pops. The next morning he came in and we couldn't wait to hear what we had. He was beaming, "It's a girl!" Bummer, we all really wanted a boy. When he followed the announcement with, "We named her Lois Patricia," I remember saying to myself, "Oh my goodness, what were they thinking, that's such a weird name."

Lois soon became my baby, I loved her so much. I was always taking her out of the crib and putting her into bed with me. As we grew up, Loie was always my partner in crime. She remains my best friend to this day.

Having an Army background, my dad was a leader in our community, a formidable personality and well respected by everyone in town. He was also a devout Catholic, and served as an usher at Sunday morning Mass. It seemed to me that in whatever he was involved, he would end up being in charge. The last fifteen years of his career he held the positions of Police and Fire Chief in our town. He was always there for whomever needed him at a moment's notice. It seemed like he was on duty 24/7, if it wasn't the phone ringing in the middle of the night, it was the fire monitor. Whether a person from the community called for medical assistance, police help or a fire, Dad would be there. He knew that the victim would feel comforted with him there. I am not actually sure if he ever got a full night's sleep in his entire adult life, but he never seemed to mind.

At home, he was a very strict disciplinarian.

Moreover, my dad was firmly committed to the status quo. He had a hard time with any changes. At age two, when his mother died, he had been passed from relative to relative. He strived to create the family structure he never had as a child and I think he was afraid of losing it. He was never abusive to any of us, he just yelled a lot; we called him a "hot headed Irishman."

I was such a quiet child that Dad's outbursts really frightened me. Every time he yelled at my mom or one of my sisters, I would run to my room and cry. One of the worst times was preparing for vacation, I usually hid till it was time to go. Packing to go to the shore was an all-day event. While at the shore we only ate out twice, other than that we brought groceries for the week. We piled into the car: two adults, four children, all the groceries, clothes, bathing suits, towels for everyone, and a portable TV. That's right, a portable TV. You could not expect my dad not to watch the news for a whole week. Needless to say, there was a lot to cram into the station wagon. *And*, it had to be perfectly level with the back seat of the car, so Dad had a clear "line of vision" out the back window. I think he packed and repacked the car fifty times before we were ready. The stress levels were immense, so I stayed in my room till it was time to go.

I remember another time when I was under five. Mom was in the hospital after having suffered a miscarriage, it was rare that my dad would be home alone with us. While he was trying to get all of us bathed and to bed, I decided it would be funny to hide from him, so I hid behind the bunk bed. At first, I remember snickering when he was calling me, thinking how funny it was for him when he couldn't find me. Well, after a minute or so, his voice got louder and he began to freak out. I became too frightened to come out from behind the bed and stayed put. Every neighbor, policeman and anyone else my dad could recruit was scouring the streets searching for me. When I was discovered, my dad was more relieved than angry, but he made me stand in the street and apologize to everyone.

As we got older, it became apparent that my sisters were much stronger than me. Not physically, but in every other way. I just didn't like conflict at all, I still don't, and will avoid it at all costs. Ann, my older sister would sometimes refer to us as countries. Jenny was Switzerland- the neutral party, Lois was France, she would fight but back down quickly, I was a Third World country, Southeast Asia or Africa- always the needy one. I grew up hearing things like this all the time. "Midgie is the needy one, Midgie is the quiet one, Midgie is the mousy one who never fights back." We three younger sisters gave Ann a country name as well... Nazi Germany-bossy and mean. It took my older sister and me years to be able to get along with each other, but I know now that I could call her, or any of my sisters for that matter, at any time, and they would drop everything to help.

My sisters and I as kids in my Grandparent's coffee shop.

My mom worked from home as a medical technician. You could usually find her sitting at the dining room table with her head bowed to a microscope. She was from a large Italian family who all lived within walking distance of our home and were all very loving and supportive of us. My mom's parents lived in the same building where they also ran a coffee shop. Pop would open the store every morning at 4:30 a.m. A group of his buddies would trickle in soon after to make the coffee and get the place ready for the day. This coffee shop was not just a regular place to get coffee, it was like home to most people who lived in Berwyn at the time. Everyone knew each other, Nan and Pop were always there, and were like parents to anyone who needed them. They fed the town, whether people could pay for the food or not. Nan made everything from scratch, any meat that was used for sandwiches was all cooked by her that morning, and sliced in the store. Everything was homemade, from soup to pasta on Wednesday nights, and the sauce too. Any grandchild she happened to be babysitting on Wednesday was in charge of forking the raviolis and turning the pasta crank. Being with my Nan and Pop was like being enveloped in a warm fuzzy blanket, your tummy full of wonderful food, and being told that you are the most perfect and precious child in the world. I think for me that is why I was so close to them. They could see that I needed that type of love and were always there to provide it.

My parents did not have a lot of money, but we never needed anything and we were very loved and happy. With the money my parents did have, they sent us to Catholic school. As I think back on my life I can actually say that my early years, when I was at Saint Monica's, were some of the most wonderful times of my life. I always felt secure at school. It was pretty much the same 32 kids, from first grade to eighth, and they were as much my family as my biological family. We celebrated every holiday together, we all went to Mass together. It was such a small, close-knit community that I knew where everyone's dad worked, and all of our parents were friends. The nuns and teachers were, for the most part, like friends to me. They were all very caring and gentle, always helping me along. Even the secretary of our school, Mrs. Hastings, was such a wonderful lady and so caring towards me. I knew if I ever needed to ask any questions or was anxious about anything she would be there.

I remember the first time I got my period, always an embarrassing time for a young girl -- but to get it in school was even worse. I went to the office and told Mrs. Hastings what happened. She told me it would be ok. She tried calling my mom, Nan, any other female relative, then my dad who was also unavailable, and finally reached my uncle at the coffee shop. In walks big Uncle Louie, a very gentle man, but not someone I wanted there on that particular day. He asked me what was wrong, Mrs. Hastings looked at me, then told him that I had a very bad stomach ache, so I would just need to go home to bed for a while. He was fine with that and took me home. I told my mom when she got home what happened, she laughed a little but was appreciative of Mrs. Hastings' quick thinking.

My early years in Catholic school and the people I encountered there not only helped to form who I have become, but also guided me toward my quest for the spiritual world around me. Many of the teachers, especially the nuns, never turned away from the questions I would ask, some even encouraged me. From as far back as I can remember, I was curious about everything spiritual; sometimes I would lay in bed at night and say the "Our Father" prayer, after every line I would ask myself what it meant. Were these truly God's words? What did he mean by "on earth as it is in Heaven"? Knowing I could ask these questions the next day, comforted me.

Sadly, Saint Monica school is not operating anymore, it has been closed, like many other Catholic schools in our area, for lack of attendance. I hope that there will still be some around for every child like I was who needed that close-knit special kind of love.

"I think I may need you as much as you need me. I don't know why this is. I guess God just places things in our hearts, and when the time is right, he lets us know."

Journal entry 4/15/07

PRESBYTERIAN CHURCH

UNTIL ABOUT ten years old my life was pretty routine. The principal at St Monica's school, Sister Regina, needed a helper in the mornings. I volunteered for the job and was pleased to have been chosen. I loved to work with Sister Regina, she was one of the nuns who encouraged me to ask questions. She was kind and patient with me, and always had thoughtful answers. Sister Regina once told me that the Lord filled her with joy, you could see the joy on her face and the confidence she had in her faith. I wish I could let her know all these years later that the things she said to me really did impact my life.

Since Sister Regina told me I could ask her anything, one day I did just that and asked what I had always wondered, "What if, when you die, there is no God and you have given your whole life up for nothing?" I know, shocking that I had the nerve to ask a nun that question but it was something I had always wanted to know. Sister Regina was so gracious; she sat down next to me and said, "Midge, there are some things in this life that we cannot see or hear or touch. Sometimes we believe anyway, and that is called faith. If you talk to God and ask Him questions as if He is your friend, just like you do with me, He will bless you. And like me, you will not only believe, but you will feel Him in your heart and know He is there. The next time you are cold, just close your eyes and ask God to be with you, to put His arms around you and keep you warm. He will." I tried it that afternoon during my walk home. I was shivering, I talked to God and asked Him to warm me, genuinely believing that He would. I was amazed, the shivers stopped and I felt Him.

I was so excited when I got home that night, I wanted tell my family about my talk with Sister Regina. My parents were not at all happy with me, here is pretty much how I remember it going. I started, "So this morning when I was helping Sister Regina, she said I could ask her anything I wanted, so I asked her, 'When she dies, if there is no God will she be sad that she wasted her whole life being a nun?'" There was dead silence, no one made a sound or moved a muscle. My dad's face blazed red, then in his booming voice while smacking his hand on the table, he bellowed, "Goddamnit, girl, don't you know better than to ask a nun a question like that? It is not your place to be asking questions!" I skipped dinner and went immediately to my room on my own without even being told. I didn't understand my dad saying it was not for us to ask questions about religion. I always felt that God wanted me to understand him, and how else could I understand without asking? That didn't stop me, I *did* ask, and continued to ask ...and I'm glad I did. Because of the answers Sister Regina gave me, not only did I talk to God and ask Him to help me, but I *felt* Him. I never had the chance to tell my parents that part, I was afraid to ever bring the subject up again. I lay on my bed and cherished the feeling of His arms around me. This began a lifetime of having conversations with God while I walked.

During 1975 the Vietnam War was at an end. Saigon had fallen, the South Vietnamese had unconditionally surrendered to the North, and our soldiers had come home. There was an operation called "Baby Lift" which evacuated over 3,300 infants and children from Vietnam on 30 flights to the US, Australia, France and Canada. Trinity Presbyterian church, across the street from my school, hosted 83 Vietnamese refugees and orphaned children from Operation Baby Lift. The refugees were hosted at the church for over two weeks. They were provided with everything needed while the church members worked to find homes for them. Trinity Presbyterian church was later awarded the Freedom Foundation's Humanitarian Activities Award for its efforts.

> "A memorable opportunity to serve was presented in 1975 when Trinity sheltered 83 refugees, many of them orphans, fleeing the collapse of South Vietnam. For over two weeks they were housed, fed, clothed, and provided

medical care while arrangements were made to match community resources with human needs. Freedoms Foundation honored Trinity and selected Rev. Bohl to receive its Humanitarian Activities Award. Subsequently, two smaller groups of Vietnamese refugees were settled and cared for in Berwyn by the church."

I didn't realize it at the time, but these people left everything behind, sometimes all their family members. All in order to find safety and freedom in a foreign country. They didn't speak the language or know the customs, but they were safe.

My friends and I were in the sixth grade and heard the Presbyterian Church needed help caring for some of the refugee children. We could not wait to help, and decided to go over after school. The room where they stayed was crowded, blankets covered the floor and people were everywhere. These people looked very different from my friends and I. We had no idea where they were from or why they were here. There were girls with children and babies like I'd heard, but I was surprised to see so many older men and women. I noticed that no young men were there, and I wondered why.

One of the women from the church asked if we would be willing to feed some of the babies. "Gladly!" We were so excited we sat down on the blankets, ready to get started. I remember thinking how absolutely beautiful their little faces were. They were so perfect, lots of black hair, beautiful brown skin and soulful eyes that looked up at me with such trust and love. I was immediately enamored. As we were sitting there I felt someone watching me. I looked around and my eyes connected with an older woman. She was sitting on the floor with a little girl in her lap; she looked like she had the weight of the world on her shoulders, but had resigned herself to bearing it. She was dressed in a worn black dress, and had long salt and pepper hair that was tied behind her head in a braid. When our eyes connected, there was a rush of emotion that I didn't expect to feel. My heart felt like it was too big for my chest, and for a moment I couldn't breathe. I smiled, but what I really wanted to do was cry. It was not pity I felt, it was a profound knowing. I felt I was somehow connected to her, but how could that be? I had no idea where she was from, I couldn't even communicate with her. I remember wanting to go and crawl into her lap, for *her* to comfort *me*. Little did I know that from that one moment, my life would be changed forever.

After my first day helping at the church I ran home. I wanted to ask my mom about these beautiful people who couldn't speak English and had come from another country with nothing but the clothes on their backs. My mom explained to me very briefly that they were from a country called Vietnam, and there was trouble in their country so they had to leave.

You may wonder how in 1975 I knew nothing about Vietnam. We were a young family with four girls who were never very interested in the news, not to mention I was only ten at the time. The only thing I can remember is overhearing things about Vietnam and "the war" and being so thankful that I didn't have a brother who had to "go to war." I kept hearing that when the boys went over there they didn't come home. War was a completely foreign concept to me.

I went early to school the next morning, I was eager to tell Sister Regina about these gentle people. I told her I felt like I knew these people, their eyes, their smiles. And even though we didn't understand each other, I felt drawn to them. When I looked in their eyes there was such a strong connection, I could feel my heart swelling. "You are a very special girl," she confided "and sometimes the Holy Spirit speaks to our hearts and places blessings there. Keep talking to Him, and pray that someday you will know the reasons."

Little did we know that was the beginning of a lifelong journey of my soul. I began to pray.

"I know this sounds weird but I can't help how I feel. I really feel like I already know you, and I am going to be reunited with you. I know God had this planned for me all along."

Journal entry 5/25/07

VIETNAM "OBSESSION"

FOR MANY years I continued to have an interest in all things Vietnam. After the war, when I was in high school, I asked every history teacher about it. I guess for most adults it was still a raw wound that had not had time to heal. Most people just skimmed over the material, not really wanting to discuss it, some were supportive, and one of my teachers brought newspapers he had kept from the war. He stayed with me after school to go over them and try to answer my inquiries. It was exciting for me to look at all of those newspapers. I had overheard pieces of information from my parents and other adults, but to actually see the articles myself was amazing. I would also go to library and look up any information they had on Vietnam. (Of course, there were no computers back then). There was not much written about it, it seemed like everyone just wanted to forget and move on.

I desperately wanted to talk to people who had been there. I wanted to know everything about Vietnam, about the war, and especially about the people and their lives. Because a local church had supported refugees and helped them settle here, I would look for Vietnamese people, but never had the courage to stop them to talk. Another source of information was American men who had been there. I knew of one soldier in our community who worked with my dad, I had overheard his story from my parents. I knew he would be fascinating to talk to, but my mom and dad forbade me to talk to him because it may have upset him.

During this time, I would stand in front of the mirror in my bedroom and hold my eyes back so they looked Asian. I would tape them there, I felt that they looked so much more natural, I wanted them to stay slanted. Good thing no one ever caught me doing that, or else I may have been committed. Vietnam, the war, the people, the land; I felt deep within that a part of me was somehow left there. I was forever searching for something. I couldn't explain it to anyone without sounding a bit crazy. I would watch documentaries about the war in Vietnam and look for anything familiar, and question "Was I there?" When I was 15 or 16 years old I learned about the Cu Chi Tunnels; I desperately wanted to explore them, I was obsessed. My friends didn't seem to get it, they were more interested in boys and going to the mall. I had fun with my friends, but wished I had someone I could talk to with the same interest, someone I could trust and not think I was looney. So much of the time I leaned on God, sometimes I could almost feel Him patting me on the shoulder saying, "All in due time, Midgie."

Years later, at a flea market I found "TIME" magazines that had cover photos of the fall of Saigon. Immediately, I bought every one that had pictures of Vietnam. I remember excitedly looking through all of them, reading the articles and searching for anything that might speak to me. It may sound crazy, but I was so convinced that I had been there before; the feeling I left something behind was so strong in me. I was constantly searching for anything that might trigger a memory or a feeling, a connection I could pursue.

I can only describe my feelings during those years as a yearning for something, but I could not grasp what it was. As I got older it did become apparent that it was not *something* I was missing but *someone*. I don't know how, but I knew it was a boy. I felt sometime in the past our souls had been connected but I lost him. This is where it got sticky for me; as a Christians was I supposed to believe that? 'No' was the answer I was always given and it was always the loudest in my head. Although, when I talked to God, He never put His hand up to me to say no, He just asked me to be patient and listen.

In the early 1990s I remember being consumed with wanting to see the Vietnam memorial in Washington,

DC. My husband at the time had no interest in this at all but finally agreed to go with me on what he referred to as my "morbid obsession weekend". Luckily for me, all he wanted to do was sit and eat his lunch while I went down to the memorial. I was humbled when I saw it for the first time. I read a plaque that described the "Operation Baby Lift" flight that crashed, killing 138 people, including 78 children and 35 crew members. I could barely breathe, I had to walk away. I sat and sobbed until I was empty, then I got up and went to find my husband. My heart ached to have someone who understood me, someone who would comprehend the emotions I was going through. It was a very quiet ride home.

4

"I have wanted you and known you would be there needing me for many, many years. Sometimes it was even hard for me to look at little faces like yours and not cry. My heart ached for the need of you."

Journal entry 4/15/07

STRANGE HAPPENINGS

I DELIBERATELY chose to go to a college four hours from home because I was painfully shy. I knew that if I stayed near home I would never leave my comfort zone. This way I *had* to break out of my shell. Anyone who knows me now will have a hard time believing I was that shy, but it was true. When my parents left me at the dorm, I sat in my room for hours crying. I struggled with the urge to call and have them return to get me. I decided to go downstairs and talk to people. I thought, *If they don't like me, I'll call my parents and leave.* After much angst, I entered the community room, approached a group of senior nursing students and asked where I could buy a soda. Well, apparently not only do they *not* use that word in northern Pennsylvania, but the way I said the "o" was very amusing to them. For the next two hours, they had me say every word they could think of that had an "o" in it. They laughed when I asked for a soda, but you should have heard the roar when I asked where I could buy a "hoagie". I was in, they officially accepted me as an honorary nursing senior. Later, they invited me to go to the local bar (the only bar in town) and I was included the following weeks in all their pranks of the new students. I felt great, the next time I went home was Thanksgiving and I haven't stopped talking since. The years I spent in college was a time of personal growth where I learned an abundance about myself and my faith.

I was very close to my grandparents and missed them terribly while at school. They were wonderful people with huge hearts, family was the center of their world. Every Sunday after church growing up, we all gathered at Nan and Pop's house. Those times formed who I became as a person. It was a time in my life I felt truly loved and cherished. While away, I phoned my Nan's house every Sunday morning to talk to everyone. My aunts, uncles and cousins would get on the phone in turn and tell me about their week. I loved hearing everyone's voice, it made me feel like I was right there. My Nan would send me letters every Sunday night and would put in a ten dollar bill. I loved her letters, even today we laugh about how she wrote them. One time she was writing while watching the Super Bowl; right in the middle of talking about my cousins, mid-sentence she writes, "Touchdown Redskins!" then goes back to finish her original thought. It encouraged me to know there were people at home who were proud of me and wanted me to succeed. Those letters and phone calls helped me remain focused each week.

One week in the winter of my last year, I had the urgent feeling that I should call my pop. But I didn't want to call, because when I spent money on phone calls during the week my Nan would send more money in her weekly letter. Periodically throughout that week while sitting in class or talking with my roommates, my heart would ache and I would think of Pop.

This particular week it was really troubling me, a little voice in my head kept saying, call Pop, call Pop. I didn't know the reasons for these feelings so I kept busy and waited for Sunday. Friday morning, I was asleep when my mom called. Pop had passed away suddenly from a heart attack in the early hours of the day. Until this moment I had never experienced the death of a loved one. This was my Pop, always there to tell me that I was perfect and beautiful. He couldn't be gone, it was not possible. The sorrow and heartbreak I felt were crippling, I curled into a ball on my bed and wept until I was empty. I was so angry with myself because I had not acted on that urge to call him. I felt I had missed out on telling him I loved him and saying good-bye one last time. Although I didn't understand it, this was my first experience with a premonition, a dream or a "psychic" feeling.

My Pop, Angelo "the Angel" Alleva knew how to live and how to die. He was always active and took pleasure in everything he did. His standard answer for anyone who asked how he was doing was "Terrrrriffic!" His passions were his family, hunting, fishing and bowling with his friends. The night he passed away he had played in a bowling tournament and won. He came home, placed the trophy on the table and went to bed.

This is my Pop. Always a smile on his face.

Three months after Pop passed, my parents had a dinner to celebrate my graduation. During the dinner my nan said to me, "I want to give you a gift from Pop and me. The week that Pop died, he was obsessed with getting this gift for you. He dragged his friend Gus to the city three different times to buy these." I was overwhelmed as she presented me with a pair of diamond earrings. "I kept telling him that he had months to buy the earrings, but he wouldn't listen. Maybe he knew something was happening, Gus said Pop was popping nitro pills all that week, but when he asked him if he was ok he would say, 'never better'. You are our first grandchild to graduate from college, he was so proud of you and really wanted you to have these for your graduation." As Nan explained this to me I realized that was the week I had wanted to call Pop but didn't. I was so touched, these earrings mean so much to me I have worn them every day since.

We still had breakfast at Nan's house every Sunday, but it was not the same without Pop. Nan maintained her work at the coffee shop and kept busy, but her joy was no longer there. She was heartbroken and became quiet from her loss. Within that year I became engaged, and we were all busy planning the wedding. As we got closer to the wedding date, Nan seemed more solemn. We didn't realize that it was not just sadness, she had become ill and had kept it from us. Nan passed away two weeks before my wedding, which was difficult. However I am fortunate she was there to help me pick out my dress and veil and I am so glad I have those special memories with her.

Newly married, I lived in my grandparents' house while we saved to buy a house of our own. Being in their house without them was challenging, I missed them and thought of them often. One night I had a dream that was so real, when I woke up I felt sure I would see my pop standing there beside me. In the dream I went down the stairs of the house and my pop was sitting there with his side to me. He wouldn't look at me but kept repeating, "We are fine, you *have* to let us go... don't be so sad, we are very happy." I didn't fully understand the dream, but it was so real that I felt a sense of responsibility to remember them with a smile and not tears. They had passed on to a better place and I knew then that they would always be a part of my life. Our souls were connected and they were watching over me. After that dream I began to realize that these feelings were not new to me, I recalled having similar feelings in my youth. I didn't yet understand these dreams and feelings that felt like ties to foreign places and people.

Lois, who is my sister and best friend, always seemed to understand me. One Christmas she gave me a book called "Requiem", a very graphic book of images from 135 Vietnam War photographers from different nations who never made it home. I loved it! I dove right in studying all the photos, as if I was searching for something, although I didn't know what that was. About two thirds through the book I flipped the page and there it was, a picture of a baby; abandoned in the center of the road surrounded by smoke, soldiers and chaos. I was so unsettled my feelings frightened me, I had to close the book. I felt like there was a hand gripping my throat, I could not stop the tears from flowing. It took years before I was able to open that book again.

Another time, Lois was treating me to the show "Miss Saigon" in Philadelphia for my birthday, I was so excited. I enjoyed the show, but what I remember most is a scene in the second half where a soldier confronts a Vietnamese girl in her home. A small boy peeks out and she quickly tells him to hide. I was so overcome with fear and sadness for that little boy and his mother, knowing they were in danger. I felt their fear, I could not handle it and ran out to the lobby. Lois came out to make sure I was okay, I told her I just needed a minute. Eventually I was able to pull myself together and return to my seat, knowing it was only a show. I felt a pain in my heart, a pain so deep, somehow knowing what that girl was feeling at that moment when her son was in danger.

I didn't understand, *why* did I have such a hard time looking at these precious faces? Experiences like this were so difficult for me. I knew it was a calling or a message, I just needed direction. I asked God to show me what to do, what was He leading me towards? All I could do was continue to have faith and trust the Lord would eventually lead me.

5

"We got a call today from Sue. She said you were born! Very healthy, 7 pounds, and you are living at the orphanage waiting for us to come get you. Sue said you were born July 11th, that's John's birthday! You have a special angel watching over you!"

Journal entry 9/25/07

WORK AND JOHN

WHEN I finished college I was nineteen years old, living at home with my family, and was hired by The Respiratory Department at our local community hospital. I loved my job, encouraging patients in the process of their healing, and comforting them in their time of need. It gave me a confidence I had never felt before and I began to believe in myself. Working at the hospital, I met people who are still in my life today that I consider more family members than friends. One very special person I met was our medical director John. I cannot say that the first time I met him I felt any kind of connection, unless you consider "fear" a connection. He was the boss, the big boss, he was a gruff and quiet man and when you first met him his presence could be intimidating. I came to know him as a gentle giant and he quickly became one of my most cherished friends. John was a very patient and caring man whose knowledge was invaluable, he was my mentor and taught me everything I needed to know to be successful at my job. He was never bothered when he had to explain things to me, he loved that I was eager to learn. We worked well together but it was so much more than that. I know we both felt there was some kind of bond that went much deeper than mere friends. From the beginning of our friendship there was an awareness between us that was only ours. When he walked into the room I could feel him there even before I saw him. There was a love and respect between us and a feeling of always having known each other; he was like a father to me, I felt so secure and loved when I was with him.

I worked night shift and John came in early every morning. Mornings were our time, we would sit and talk about work, patients, whatever was on our minds. As soon as I heard the doors of ICU open at 5:45a.m. I would run to greet him, and have his coffee waiting for him. Many mornings John would bring donuts for the staff, when he did he always brought a Boston cream donut just for me, even delivering it in its own bag. It was sweet of him and he was excited to have that donut. The funny thing is, I loved cream donuts but did not like the chocolate on top. I would thank him for making me feel special, then without him seeing, I would scrape off all the chocolate and eat the donut. Whenever I see a Boston cream donut now, I laugh to myself and know that John is laughing with me. John was a great chef too, at parties he would cook his famous egg rolls or pasta sauce. Once he tasted Nan's homemade pasta and sauce he wanted to replicate it. We joked that he could never get his to taste like my grandmother's. Nan shared her recipe, but John thought she must be holding back some hidden secret of the family pasta sauce.

One day in his office I noticed John's certificates of internships in four different specialties. On closer inspection, I discovered there was a four-year lapse between 1969 and 1973. When I asked John about the gap, he said he was in Vietnam. It sparked an immediate reaction in me. Although we had worked together for a year, I knew nothing about this. I immediately wanted to know everything, and peppered him with questions about Vietnam. He responded quietly and with some hesitance that he was a Navy commander and worked as both a medic and surgeon there. He said there was so much pain, destruction and constant fear. He had no good memories of that time or of anything positive in Southeast Asia. Clearly there were not many memories he was willing to share. Disappointed but not wanting to push him on the subject, I rarely asked again. He didn't understand my desire to know about that distant place. I said, "I don't know why I want to go there someday, but as far back as I can remember I've felt somehow connected to the people and the land and I want to adopt a baby boy from there."

He shook his head sadly, looked at me and said, "I never saw anything of beauty in that country and have no desire to return." I hugged him then, it was hard to see this big intense man who was so well respected by everyone, seem to physically shrink and close himself off when he talked about it.

It was about that time I married a guy I met while I was in college just a year and a half before. I was very young, twenty years old, not even old enough to have a drink at my own wedding. We bought a house that was almost an hour drive from my parents, my work and my friends. I hated living so far away from everyone

PICTURE COURTESY OF BENJAMIN WILLENS

John S. Willens, commander US Navy

but this was the house my husband wanted. There were times when I felt isolated, I wasn't able to be with my mom or family unless I had another reason to drive there. Unfortunately, I was not strong enough at that point in my life to speak up or go against him. Early in the marriage, I did talk to my husband about my interest in Vietnam, my desire to adopt and my feelings that I may have been there in some other lifetime. He was not receptive to these ideas at all, he didn't like to hear any of "that hocus pocus crap" or my "morbid obsession" but my desire never dimmed. When I finally had my first child we named him Richard John, for both grandfathers. I called work after the delivery and everyone already knew about the baby. They said John was so happy, going around telling everyone who would listen that the baby was named after him. If you know anything about hospitals, you know how the rumors spread. Well, they were flying around that day. I had my daughter Paige four years later, she was the most beautiful baby with mops of black hair and porcelain skin. I must tell you she is still that beautiful today! After Paige was born, things started to go south with my marriage. My husband Rich, never liked my work or the people there. He didn't want anyone influencing me, but my friends and co-workers had always been there for me. Everything was stressful at this time. Rich and I did manage to go to counseling one time. He said he hated everything about my work. It was easy for the counselor to make the connection, it was because I was liked and respected at work. Rich promptly walked out of the appointment and we never went back.

John had gotten very ill that year and his health was declining quickly. My husband would not allow me to go down to visit John unless I had to work. He said it was a waste of gas. I was torn, I was still not strong enough to stand up to him at this point in my life. Rich knew how close I was to John and seemed very jealous of that relationship. Perhaps because he didn't understand it. When I got the call that John passed away on August 15th, 1996, I just remember sitting on my kitchen floor and crying. It was an emptiness and sorrow that filled me to my core. He was such a beautiful person and when he passed I felt like I lost a piece of my heart. I know I had never felt such a loss and never have since. To this day, I miss him so much and talk to him all the time like he is right there next to me. I just wish I could hear his side of the conversation.

John's death was a tipping point, I deeply resented not being there for him at the end. Rich and I had been having problems for a while but after John died, I thought, *I can't live with this anymore.* I think a lot of our problems rooted from the fact that I was so young when we married. Over time, I had figured out who I was, what I wanted in a marriage, and what kind of life I wanted for my kids. I did not want to stay together "for the kids" and show them that it was okay to live with fear and anger all the time. I packed up everything and finally left on January 2nd, 1997. My friend Betsy came up to the house and we literally packed up the Christmas ornaments off the tree, all the kids' clothes and important things and we moved to my mom and dad's. I think I was finished in the marriage way before I actually left. For nine months Rich and I were basically still married but separated under the same roof. We had not been speaking for a while and that Christmas was not very good. When you and your kids are locked in the bedroom on Christmas morning, and your seven year old looks up and says, "Mommy, we have to get out of here, I'm scared" you know it's over and it's past time to go.

When the kids and I moved in with my parents it was such a sense of relief, we were all safe and together. While we were living there my dad got very ill. I was glad to have been there at the time to be able to be with my mom and support her through Dad's illness. He passed away shortly after. Needless to say I felt like it was one loss after another, and I felt especially bad for my children. My dad was quite a stoic man who had a very difficult time expressing his feelings. The first time I ever heard him say, "I love you" was to my son Richie. He was finally able to express his love through his grandchildren. Rich was seven years old and had been very close to my dad. He idolized him and spent much of his early years under my dad's desk at the police station playing, then having lunch with him. He used to tell everyone he was going to be in the Army like Poppop, and then he was going to be Police Chief when Poppop retired. My son Rich did eventually join the Army just like his Poppop.

This is my Dad and Rich.
Rich was so proud to be wearing a
uniform, just like his Poppop.

People ask me if I wish I hadn't gotten married so young and my answer is always the same. I think we live our lives and make decisions that we have to stick by and learn from, no regrets, ever! My years being married helped me to learn who I was. I discovered I was strong.

There was so much change in our lives. All I could do was continue to pray.

UBND PHƯỜNG ĐẠI NÀI T.P HÀ...
CHỨNG THỰC BẢN SAO ĐÚNG VỚI BẢN CHÍNH
Số chứng thực 1306 Quyển số 01/...
Ngày 14 tháng 11 năm 2007
CHỦ TỊCH

Xác nhận của Bệnh viện

Trưởng khoa

"I thank God everyday for your Daddy. Without him, not only would I not be able to go through this, but I would not be the person I am today. Daddy gives me the strength to believe in who I am and to believe in my dreams. Sometimes they come true!"

Journal entry 5/28/07

DECISION TO ADOPT

A FEW months after my dad passed, the kids and I moved into a charming house on the next street over from my mom. I was on my own really for the first time ever. My boss and friend Mary worked with me on scheduling, and my mom was a huge help watching the kids. I honestly don't think I could have done it without her, and I would like to think it also helped her, having the kids around and not being alone.

I had started to take Richie to Karate the previous year to help with anger issues from the tension we were experiencing at home. When I saw how great it was for him, I decided to join as well. This is where I discovered my own strength, both mental and physical. The classes were small and many of us became friends. We would occasionally go out after class, this was a new group of friends that supported me and helped me grow as a person. Dave, one of the students, and I became close and enjoyed spending time together. I felt like I could talk to him about anything, he was very supportive when my dad got sick and we began to date soon after.

He was such a kind, gentle and loving man, I found him easy to fall in love with. He treated me like a partner and a friend and we shared everything.

One weekend, Dave and I decided to take the kids to the Philadelphia Art Museum. It was a great day and the kids were having a ball. We discovered it had been raining for quite some time when we came out. At the bottom of the "famous" art museum steps there was a puddle that was the size of a small pool. My kids froze, terrified. They were never allowed to be wet or muddy when they were with their father, and they could not imagine how they were going to get to the car that was down the steps and across the street, without getting wet and muddy. They looked at me and I said it would be fine, then they looked at Dave with fear in their eyes. I am not sure if Dave understood the impact his next move would make in their lives and mine. He jumped down the steps, ran into the puddle and started jumping and splashing around. Then he looked up and said to the kids, "Come on, what are you guys waiting for?" They were thrilled, and couldn't believe that a grown up would do that, and let *them* do it too. I was delighted as I watched my kids act like kids, and I was very grateful for the experience.

This time in my life was one of self-discovery and renewal. I was taking care of a house, job and family. It gave me time to think and learn and eventually come to *know* that I was able to do it all on my own. One weekend while reflecting, I had come to the conclusion that I was a very strong woman, and I could handle pretty much anything I needed to on my own.

That weekend Dave and I went for a walk at what had become our special place. Near our house there was a farm and pasture, a big barn, a quiet path, and a decrepit bridge over a stream. I remember telling him, "I feel good and strong and *free!* For the first time in my life, I get it, I know I am going to be OK. I feel like I can do anything." That was when Dave turned to me and asked me to marry him. Dave, true to form, had no ring, just us and his spur of the moment proposal. Here I was just two seconds ago, telling him all this about doing things on my own and being free, and he proposes. I was elated! Then I thought, *I was just going on about not needing anyone else, I hope he didn't hear me.* Of course I said yes. I was happy I could do everything on my own, but it's better to enjoy it all with your best friend by your side. He later said that he was waiting for me to get to the point where I was strong enough to be on my own before he asked me. He is still my best friend and understands me like no one else. I really feel like he was meant to be a part of my life.

●   ●   ●

"Our 'special place', the bridge my kids think looks like a scene from a horror movie."

When we sat the kids down to tell them about the proposal, Paige was ecstatic. She was five and her only thought was that she could wear a great dress. Richie ran out of the room. I took him aside to talk; he said he felt like it was just so final. I guess there was always that little part of him that just wanted everything, as bad as it had been, to go back to normal. I have heard a saying that it is easier to live with what you know than to face the unknown. I told him I would not do this unless we were all in it together. He said he loved Dave and was really happy that we would all be a family. We were married five months later. I walked down the aisle with Richie on one side of me and Dave's dad, with whom I had become very close, on the other. Paige was the flower girl and wore a beautiful white dress. She said "*We* are marrying Dave, not just you, Mommy." I do have to mention that the white dress for Paige was the first of five different outfits she picked to wear that day. Periodically during the party, she would run inside, then come out with something fabulous on to impress the crowds. Definitely a fashion diva from the start, and she remains one to this day.

Dave loved my kids and always treated them as his own. A few years after we were married, someone at school told Paige that Dave was not her *real* father, and her younger brother and sister were not her *real* siblings. Paige was devastated and asked Dave if he would adopt her and Rich. She said that he had been her dad since she was four years old, and he was the one that was always there for her. He helped her with her homework, yelled at her to clean her room, and did everything else a dad is supposed to do. She wanted to be adopted and have the same name as Dave, me, and the kids. A few months later it was done, Dave had adopted them as his own. To this day when people comment that Paige looks like her dad (Dave) she just smiles and agrees, "Yep, I do."

Within the first two years of our marriage we welcomed our first child together. Keegan was, from the beginning, such a bright beautiful child. He not only looked just like Dave, but he acted just like him. He was forever deconstructing things, just to see if he could put them back together, or to get parts for other projects. We used to joke that we did not have one toy in our house that was not broken apart and remade into something else. After having Keegan, I thought God was truly leading me toward adoption. From the beginning of our relationship, Dave was aware of my feelings about adoption from Vietnam. He was very supportive. Vietnam was open to adoption with the US and I was seeing signs everywhere that this was what I was meant to do. We were at a family function where I met a woman who, when we began talking, told me she worked in foreign adoptions, especially with Vietnam adoptions. I saw this as a sign. I was so excited, I told her of my lifelong feelings of wanting to adopt specifically from Vietnam. She said there was a meeting the next week going over everything needed to begin the process of adoption. I discussed this with Dave and he agreed it would be a good idea to go and find out any information I could.

I came home from that meeting so excited to adopt. I was sure this was exactly where God wanted me to be. There is a funny saying that I have found to be so true, just when you think you have made all the best plans, if you listen closely you might hear God laughing. He may just have other plans for you.

Later that same week, I was due to give plasma. I went every month to donate plasma. It is a two hour procedure where they take blood from one arm, separate it and re-infuse the red cells into your other arm. I didn't mind the procedure and it was a small thing I could do to be able to help others in need. The month before, I had gone and since I didn't have a regular menstrual cycle, they asked me to do a pregnancy test prior to my next appointment so they could have a confirmation that I was not pregnant for the chart. So I bought the triple kit at Costco. Later that day I did one of the tests and lo and behold, it was positive. I couldn't believe it! So after doing the other two tests in the pack just to make sure this was correct, I sat down and sighed. What is this, Lord? I thought you were leading me to adopt, I thought that was the road I was supposed to be on. Here I was, all set to make my dream of adoption come true, and I was pregnant. Not just pregnant, but I found out later that week, four months pregnant. I felt guilty for the feelings that I had, I am sorry to say that I was a little bit confused and disappointed. For someone who in the past had to use fertility drugs and had so many problems getting and staying pregnant, this was a huge shock. I was sad and I know that sounds terrible, but sitting at my kitchen table looking at my seven month old baby in a bouncy seat, I just didn't know what to feel. It should have been elation, but it wasn't. When I told Dave he was very excited. I don't think adoption even crossed his mind then. But for me I had to let this all sink in. I had to have some pretty direct conversations with God to please make Himself more clear in the future. When I told my mom, she was thrilled. Another little one to love, what could be better? When I told her I wasn't sure if I was ready to do this all over again she said, "Sure you are, Midgie, it was all meant to happen this way. This one will be your special blessing from God Himself." So we put the adoption on hold for a while and six months later on June 7th, 2001, I gave birth to a beautiful baby girl, Erin Theresa, who is truly to this day, a gift from God Himself.

I remember sitting in the hospital with my three children around me and my new baby in my arms looking at Dave and saying, "It is still there, I still want to adopt." Poor Dave, he just shook his head and said, "Let's just see where life brings us." I can imagine what his thoughts were at that moment in time. Unfortunately, in 2003 Vietnam closed its doors to adoptions with the US. The devastation I felt when it was first announced, was like a jolt to my core. I was completely heartbroken. I had been following the news, but knowing that there was no possibility now to adopt was like a door slamming shut in my face. In the world of international adoptions, the question of whether a baby or child is abandoned is perhaps the most significant question. There were so many investigations by the State Department of children and babies as to whether they were actually abandoned, or if their mother or family was coerced or bribed into giving them up. Overall I think it was an honest system, but for officials, it was a very serious matter, and they did not want to take any chances of problems later, so the doors were shut between Vietnam and the US. Later, I learned of all the families that had started the adoption process and had been over there to meet their children, now their children were there and they did not know if or when they would ever be able to go over and get them. I stopped feeling sorry for myself and began to pray for these children and their families instead.

The doors of Vietnam opened again for adoptions to the US in 2005 with a three year agreement. Both countries agreed that it was in the best interest of the children to reopen. The day they reopened I begged my husband to consider adopting. He knew that this was something I was very passionate about, but he really felt that it would be too much. At this point in our lives, we had four children ages 17, 13, 5 and 4. He suggested trying to channel that passion into something else. Maybe working with children or families at the church. I had to agree, this is not something that one person can just run out and do. It has to be a joint decision, and both parties have to be passionate about it. So I prayed for strength and guidance.

I didn't bring the subject up again for a year or so, but in early 2007 the feelings were so strong that I couldn't sleep. I would get up at night, come down to the computer and cry for hours while looking at adoption sites and those beautiful little faces. It was heartbreaking. I finally decided I had to ask Dave one more time. If his answer was no, I would find some way to get over the loss. But at least I figured there would be a definite decision one way or another. I was very nervous to talk to him. Not because I was in any way afraid of him, I was just afraid that if the answer was no, could I handle the disappointment? I spoke with my friend Betsy who I had been friends with since I had started working at Paoli. She knew both Dave and I pretty well, and had a knack for being able to look at things with an outside view. She said that Dave understands me and knows how I feel about this. If I am honest with him, we would be able to work it out no matter which way it went. She also said that respect goes both ways, and if he is not on board, I would have to respect his feelings.

When we spoke that night I was very honest with him. I told him that as he knew, I had these feelings my whole life and I firmly believe that I was not only meant to, but I didn't believe I could make it through this life without finding this child. It was the ache of an empty spot in my heart that I just couldn't seem to fill. He took a deep breath and said that, knowing this was a passion of mine, he would not only agree to do it, but also make it his passion, and he would be honored to take this journey with me. I felt a warm rush of relief, thankfulness and elation welling up in me. Lots of tears later we went to bed, but before I drifted off I said a little prayer to thank God for this man beside me, someone so selfless that he would be willing to go through this process for me. I also talked to my friend John and told him I was finally doing this. I knew his experiences were not very good in Vietnam, but he knew my attraction to it, and the feelings I had about finding that little boy, and I really wanted him to be with me on this journey.

7

"I told Daddy yesterday that I can't wait to hold you and feel you against me. I already love you and I don't even know if you have been born yet. I pray for you every day, and for your birth mom, that she feels Gods love and has a peacefulness in knowing you will be loved."

Journal entry 4/16/07

ADOPTION PROCESS

OUR JOURNEY, or rather, whirlwind adventure, began the next morning when I contacted my friend Sue. Sue is a social worker and our liaison for adoption. She knew my desire to adopt and said she could help us get started when we were ready. Sue assisted us through the preliminary process and contacted her friend RoseMarie, who was the agent for adoptions in Vietnam. She sent me a packet of papers and also had me call the home study agency. She said to fill the paperwork out as soon as I could, but don't neglect my children to get it done. I dove right in and didn't leave the kitchen table or raise my head from the papers for three days until they were complete and ready to go back. The process had really begun, I was one step closer to finding my baby.

Easter Sunday was the next weekend, Dave and I decided to tell our families and close friends that day. Not everyone understood our reasons, we already had four kids and some didn't understand why we would want to adopt. But those who truly knew me followed up the news with "Wow, it's really happening? It's about time!"

It was a very busy time in our lives. We had one child graduating from high school, one going into high school, and two in elementary school. It seemed like there wasn't enough time in the day to get everything done. Dave and I had to go to a class given by the home study office about raising children. At first we laughed, here we were, parents of four going to a class on how to raise kids. The class turned out to be very informative and we did learn a lot. There are many things when adopting children from another country that I didn't think about. The child is not used to you, your look, your smell, your food, or your language; it is all very different to them. Sometimes the baby may need an adjustment period for getting used to you. The one thing they didn't mention and I didn't think about is the adjustment period *you* as parents may need. When you adopt, you are meeting a child for the first time. He may be newborn, a couple of months old, or a toddler. You don't really know him at all. You don't know what makes him happy, sad, or what comforts him. You just fumble through and love him till you figure it all out.

It really felt like everything was moving along well. In August 2007 we finally met RoseMarie face to face at an adoption conference in Philadelphia. We learned about international travel and met other families who had adopted children from Vietnam. We had a great dinner at a Vietnamese restaurant and enjoyed meeting the other families. After dinner we talked to RoseMarie; Dave and I had decided that if the situation presented itself, we would be willing to adopt siblings or twins. During the conversation she just looked at me and smiled, "Why don't we just wait and see what happens." My heart leapt in my chest, I knew something was happening. The next month I found out what she meant.

It was September 2007, nine o'clock in the evening. I was just getting the little kids to bed when the phone rang. It was Sue, she was very excited to tell us that we had a baby. It was a healthy baby boy who was born on July 11th. I think my heart stopped for a second when she said the date of his birth. I asked Sue to repeat it, she said he was born in a hospital in Ha Tinh, Vietnam, on July 11th, 2007. I was so shocked, I felt like all of a sudden I couldn't hear what Sue was saying, my mind just stuck on that date. That was John's birthday. I had to hand the phone to Dave, I started to cry tears of joy. I knew right then that John *did* know I was adopting and he was with us on this journey. It was like getting a little hug from him, letting me know he was here with me. We waited so long, it seemed like an eternity, we didn't get the official papers and the first pictures of the baby until November 2007.

RoseMarie could not tell us what she knew about the baby in August when we saw her because of the strict policies for international adoption; there has to be at least 60 days from when a baby is brought into the orphanage, during which time they try to find any family who will claim the baby.

Looking back, I'm amazed at all of the "coincidence". In July, RoseMarie told us that our paperwork was there, complete and approved. The next baby boy brought to the orphanage would be ours, but we may have to wait a bit, because it's unusual for boys to be abandoned. Well, we found out later that Brodey was not only the next baby boy in the orphanage, but he was the next baby in the orphanage. I feel like this was all meant to be, like it was all in God's big plan from the beginning. After all of the "I's" were dotted and the "T's" were crossed, Brodey was officially up for adoption and we said yes! As soon as the pictures came through on the computer and I saw his little face, I knew immediately it was him. It was like a rush of emotion filling my heart with such immediate love and peace. I was overflowing with so much joy I was about to burst. I had finally found him, the little piece of my soul that I always knew was missing.

I feel like our adoption process was very smooth and quick compared to other horror stories I have heard. Some friends of mine had adopted domestically and abroad, and their waiting period was very long and drawn out.

We broke the news to our friends and families on Easter Sunday April 8th, 2007 and we had Brodey in our arms April 14, 2008. That's not to say there was no pain involved. We found out about Brodey and accepted him in September 2007, we were supposed to travel to get him in November of 2007. All our paperwork was in and completed. We got a call from RoseMarie in October 2007, she said the government wanted us to have another paper called the I-600, completed prior to travel.

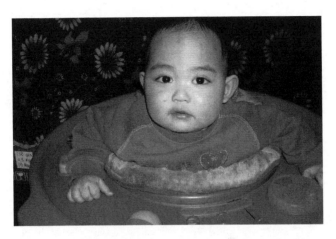

This is the first official picture of Brodey 4 months old.
We received it Thanksgiving Day 2007

(This form is used to classify an orphan, habitually resident in a non-Hague Convention country, who is or will be adopted by a U.S. citizen as an immediate relative of the U.S citizen to allow the child to enter the United States. The petition is filed by the U.S. citizen who is adopting the child.)

RoseMarie said even though this pushed our travel time back a bit, it is much better to have the I-600 completed prior to travel. God forbid you get there, get the baby then something goes wrong and you can't get the I-600. You would have to wait in country for it to be completed. This news devastated me. We knew it is for the best, but now we had a baby waiting for us in Vietnam, growing and learning without me. There was nothing left to do but wait and pray.

Once I knew that they would be contacting me via email, I checked every morning at 5 a.m. As the days and weeks went by it became harder and harder to wait. I really thought that after Christmas and the New Year, we would definitely hear. They said it would be 60 days at the most. Well, 60 days came and went, then the Holidays in our country, then came Tet, which is the Vietnamese New Year. This is the biggest holiday in Vietnam, and the whole country of Vietnam shuts down for a week to celebrate. The wait was killing me. Finally one morning in March, there was an email from the Justice Department in Vietnam with the subject line "I-600". I just sat there afraid to open it. What if it said we were not approved or some papers were not completed that needed to be? My heart was pounding and my hands were beginning to sweat. I did eventually open it, we were completely approved and ready to travel! Looking back at the timeline of the whole process I say to myself, "It really wasn't that long" but I have to tell you that every morning I did *not* get an email from them was like a knife to my heart. Knowing your baby is there, waiting for you, being cared for and loved by someone else was very painful. But it was time to move forward. We had all the paperwork we needed, we were packed and ready to go. Dave and I were booked to leave the 11th of April.

I was not in the least nervous about getting Brodey, I was, however, nervous about leaving my other kids. They would be staying with my mom so I knew they would be in good hands, and we set up a Skype account so we could talk and see them every day.

Eventually, all of the kids were very excited about adopting, but that was not how they felt when we first brought it up. I think the general reaction from them was shock. Why are we adopting when we already have kids? They didn't really understand. Once I explained the reasons and it sunk in, Paige was ecstatic, this was so exciting for her. Rich was kind of indifferent to it all. He was away at school, so his only concern was that we would have this little one that would not really know him because he would only be around in the summer. Keegan, well, I don't really know how Keegan felt. He just always seemed to go with the flow. Erin was a little nervous, she was the baby of the family, and my baby. She was afraid that with a new little one, she would be lost in the shuffle. I tried to reassure her but she was only truly reassured after seeing Brodey for the first time, and knowing that nothing and no one could ever change the way I felt about her.

There was one other thing that I was nervous about that I had never told anyone. I did eventually tell Dave because I knew he understood my quirkiness. My feeling of having been to Vietnam before, and having left someone behind was so strong in me that I was almost afraid of how I would feel being in that country. It actually wasn't a real physical fear, more of a curiosity. If I had been there before, would any of those past feelings come through. There had been places I had been to for the first time before, where I felt I had known it in a past life. One of those places was in Ireland. Of course, I dare anyone to sit on a mountain or rocky outcrop in Ireland looking out to the sea and not feel something, but I felt "at home". The only way to explain it was that it felt like I was away for a long time, and had finally come home. My fear with going to Vietnam was, what if they were not good feelings I had when I got there? We would just have to wait and see.

"Everyone will be praying for us as we travel to bring you home. I feel like I have been waiting my whole life for this. I know once I am able to hold you in my arms, my heart will be whole."

Journal entry 1/13/08

VIETNAM TRIP

IF YOU have ever traveled very long distances before, you know how difficult it can be. I had been packed for a while, some might say the minute I heard about Brodey. Fortunately our agent had a travel packet for us, so I could check and recheck everything I needed to bring. The point is, I was very ready to go when the word came that we could travel. We boarded our plane in New York City at JFK airport. The first leg of our journey was from New York to Thailand. Eighteen hours on a plane. Most people sleep on these long flights, but I was so excited that I couldn't sleep. I do believe most of the flight, I was the only one awake. Once we landed in Thailand, there wasn't much time before we had to board another plane for Hanoi. This was only a two hour flight, so as hard as it was to board another plane, it went very quickly. Flying up to Hanoi was amazing. Looking out to see all the mountains, how green everything was. It all looked so beautiful and peaceful.

The nerves didn't kick in till we landed in Hanoi. We got through customs, found our luggage, then down to meet with Chau. Chau is the in country assistant to RoseMarie. When we found him, we were surprised to also find RoseMarie. She was so organized and we felt that everything was very taken care of. The big moment was here. I was headed out the door onto Vietnamese soil. Drum roll please. It was hot. Very, very hot and humid. No weird feelings, no weird memories, just hot.

Driving to the hotel in the van is when the feelings came. It is a city, a big city with people everywhere. But even driving through the city looking out at everything there is a feeling of family. I hadn't even interacted with anyone yet, but the feeling was so strong it warmed my heart and made me smile.

When we got to the hotel, we were surprised to see that the rooms were very big, with beautiful king sized beds and wood floors. It was immaculately clean and even though there were no air conditioners, the room was cool because the windows were big and there was always a breeze blowing through. We freshened up and wanted to explore but had no idea where to begin. Dave wandered down to the street while I showered. He discovered the best kept secret in Hanoi. There was a young girl on the sidewalk across the street from the hotel; she had a hot plate, eggs, and the best baguettes in the world. She made him two egg sandwiches on baguettes. When he brought them to the room I was surprised to see it looked like a normal sandwich on a roll. I don't know what

I was expecting when he said he bought some food on the sidewalk. It was the best egg sandwich I have ever tasted. When I asked him how much it cost, he said for two of them, it was 10,000 dong. I thought that sounded like a lot of money, but when Dave converted it for me it was about thirty cents per sandwich.

When we went downstairs in the hotel, we met another couple, Stacy and Kristi, who were also in our adoption group. They had been to Vietnam several times in the past, and had adopted from there before. They were pros at getting around this city. When the four of us walked out the front door of the hotel, there were motorbikes across the street with a man on each bike asking if we needed a ride. So Kristi flagged the guys on the bikes over. I was not sure at that point what we were doing. "Stick with me" said Kristi, "it will be fine." So there we went, all four of us flying around Hanoi on the back of these bikes. The driver spoke no English and I didn't speak Vietnamese, so I was hoping he understood he was supposed to follow the others. It ended up being our preferred mode of transportation while we were in the city. It was great riding around the city. So much to see, such a different culture.

The next morning we went to breakfast at a restaurant which was on the top floor of the hotel. In the hotel, every day they would take your laundry and have it back to you the next day. This was very convenient, so Dave and I paid the little bit extra it was to have our laundry done. Since there are no clothes dryers in Hanoi because electricity is so expensive, we could sit and eat our breakfast while looking over the city through one set of windows, and our laundry hanging on a line on the roof of the hotel through the other windows!

At breakfast that second day, we met the other couples who were in our group. It is strange meeting people for the first time, hearing all their stories and not realizing that you would be connected to these people through your children for life. After breakfast we were met by RoseMarie to travel to the train station. This would be the first of two days of travel to get to the orphanage. We boarded what appeared to be a very rustic train. All kinds of people were boarding the train. There were businessmen with suits and briefcases, women carrying crates of chickens, and young women with children. The train didn't have regular seats like trains here do, it had separate rooms each with wooden bunks. There was a hallway outside the rooms, with windows out the other side of the train. We picked a room with four bunks and all settled down to get to know each other better. Wow, what an adventure. Outside my window, I could see we were leaving the city and everything was so lush and green. There were fields or I guess rice paddies with people working in them with water buffalo. I don't know why that seemed funny to me. I guess I thought it was a difficult way to work the fields, that there had to be an easier way, but for these people it was their everyday life.

Some parts of this trip were very amusing. The ride was six hours long I had to use the restroom. I asked where the ladies room was, and was shown to a room with an open door to the hallway. There was nothing except a window, a pole with two footprints on either side, and a hole in the floor with the tracks going by underneath. After standing and staring for a few minutes and trying to figure all this out, I had to wonder if this was really worth it. Well, we were two hours into the ride and I really had to go. So, I guess when in Vietnam, do as the Vietnamese. So I got myself ready, placed my feet on either side of the pole, held on, leaned back and there you have it. I tinkled on a train in Vietnam with no door, no privacy, and literally no toilet, and the whole of the country rolling by outside the window. When I came back to the room, not any worse for the wear, physically anyway, my husband was also just coming from the other direction. I asked him where he had been. To the restroom, he said. "Oh, wasn't it weird, with no door and the pole and everything." He had no idea what I was talking about. After much laughter we figured out that there was a "Western" restroom in the opposite direction than I went, and it had a door, a toilet that you could sit on, a sink and privacy! In places all over Asia they have what are called "squat potties". It is just a hole in the ground or in this case in the train floor where you are supposed to squat over the hole to do your business. The pole is there for you to hold onto if you don't have good balance. I'm not sure I will ever live this down, but everyone did get a laugh out of it.

The train brought us to a city called Vinh. We were to stay in Vinh overnight, then board a bus for a one hour ride to the orphanage in the morning. We all decided to go to our rooms to freshen up then meet for dinner in the hotel restaurant. Once downstairs, we were seated at one long table and given menus. When the waiter came to take our order, he heard us speak and asked if we were "US" and we said yes. He promptly removed our menus and gave us new ones..... with higher prices. RoseMarie, who had been through this before, refused to order from those menus, and we did get our original menus back.

There were some interesting choices for dinner. I don't think anyone at our table chose the daily special of snakehead hotpot with snake skin chips. But my husband did go out on a limb and order goat. I believe I ordered vegetables and rice, (not very adventurous) the last thing I needed the next day was to have to use the restroom on the bus ride, I was afraid of what exactly I would find there!

The next morning we woke early to a beautiful day. It was a bit daunting, this was the day we would meet our baby. It was at once exciting, emotional and terrifying. Before we left the room I sat on the bed and said a prayer that everything would go as planned that day. Then, I thanked Dave for walking this path and taking this journey with me.

We boarded the bus and started the last leg of the journey. The ride was amazing. We drove through farmlands with a background of mountains. There was so much of what we call poverty, but it seemed that these people were happy just living and working in their lives. The ride was about an hour. Suddenly the bus slowed and made a left turn. We pulled up to a fence with a small sign on it. It was written in Vietnamese but at the very bottom, there in English was the word orphanage.

The entranceway to the orphanage and the sign.

My heart was pounding. Someone came out to open the gate for us. We were all so excited we were clamoring to get a view of anything and everything around us. When the bus stopped we all wanted to run off and get to our babies, but that's not how things worked. We were led into the office part of the orphanage. There we met Mr. Dao, the man who ran the orphanage. Mr. Dao was a funny little man who appeared to be in his 40s and had a giant smile that looked like it was always on his face. He seemed to have a bright energy about him, like he not only loved his job but also loved life.

There was lots of bowing and shaking hands as we entered the office. When we went in we saw a big room with a large table and chairs all around it. The one wall of the room was covered with pictures of babies and families who have adopted them from years past. It was so nice to see that they kept pictures the families sent to them and that they liked to follow the progress of the children. Mr.Dao was so excited to meet us and wanted to get to know each couple. We were asked to sit and have tea and treats. We were all so anxious that at this point that no one wanted to eat. RoseMarie explains that we will get the babies eventually, but they have spent a lot of time and money on these treats, as is their custom to welcome us, and it would be rude to not partake. So we all sat and Mr. Dao asks where each of us was from. Mary goes first saying she was from California, and Mr. Dao was very excited about this. The two places in the states that everyone in Vietnam was familiar with are California and New York. The two other couples are from Georgia and Illinois, and it was evident he had no idea where they were so he just nodded. When he gets to us we say Pennsylvania, and I knew he would not know where that was so I followed with "it's close to New York", he was very excited about that and says, "yes, New York City!" Then he wanted to know which couple would get which baby. Again we were last. After the three girl babies, he got to us and beamed. He was so excited and proud to tell us all about our "big boy". He was the little prince of the orphanage, he was nine months old and weighed twenty-two pounds! Mr. Dao told us that it was a good thing we were there because it was getting hard for

Ba, Brodey's caretaker to carry him around. Since Brodey was one of very few boy babies in the orphanage, and he was the oldest one in the baby house, he was like a little celebrity. Mr. Dao lead Dave and I to a framed picture hanging in the office. Just a month before, a newspaper was doing an article on Mr. Dao and the orphanage because of how well it was run. The orphanage was also building a new facility with screens in the windows. Mr. Dao was very proud to tell us this, as screens are a rare commodity in Vietnam. When the newspaper people came, they took a picture of Mr. Dao, some of the caretakers, and Brodey, because he was so big and strong. I was excited to see the picture, but what I really wanted was to get to the baby.

Photo of the picture hanging in the orphanage, taken for the news paper.

Ok, the time had come. We were to walk across the yard to the baby house. This was a little one room building that housed the babies in the orphanage and their caretakers.

Here we were at the moment I had been waiting for my whole life. As we walked over I had to suppress the urge to push over everyone in front of me to get in there. Dave and I were the last to enter. As we entered I could see the caretakers, they were each holding a baby and each new Mom was going toward their baby. I was looking around, I didn't see my baby. I began to panic a little until RoseMarie pointed over to the corner of the room on our right. There on a pallet by herself was an older woman, crying while she pushed a cradle with her foot, in the cradle is my baby. She motions for us to come over. All of a sudden I'm not sure what I should do. I feel like an intruder. This was the woman who had loved and cherished my baby for nine months, and she knew we were here to take him away. As much as I wanted to hold that sleeping baby, my heart was breaking for this woman. She then motioned for me to pick him up. I did, and when I got him to my chest the feeling of total completeness overwhelmed me, I couldn't hold back the tears. Just then, he popped his little head up and looked around. He reached for Ba, his caretaker. I don't think she could help herself so she took him back and buried her face in his neck, then gathered herself and handed him back to me. As she did this she tapped my shoulder, saying "Mother" in Vietnamese so Brodey would know it was ok. He was not convinced right away, but acclimated pretty quickly when he saw all the toys we had for him. It was very difficult to be sitting with a woman who had been like a mother to your son for nine months, and you cannot communicate with her. It was breaking my heart watching her, so emotional wiping silent tears from her face and so loving towards him. I wanted her to know that Brodey would be going to a home with lots of siblings and love. I took pictures from my bag of our other kids. With these pictures were the pictures I was sent of Brodey, in some of them she was holding him. She had never seen these pictures and was so overwrought when she saw them, I motioned for her to keep them. She beamed, and held the pictures to her chest, then kissed them and placed them in her little box that held all her most treasured items. I had no idea that something so small, could be such a treasure to her.

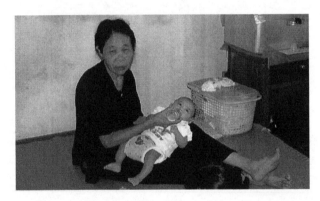

These are some early photos we received from RoseMarie of
Brodey at 7weeks with Ba

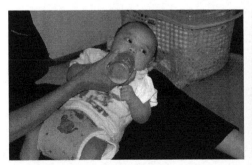
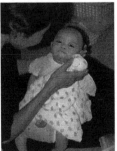

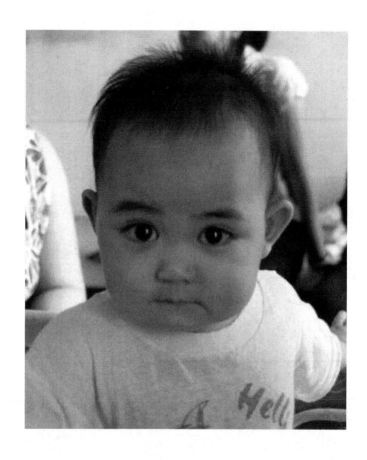

Brodey the day we first met

Brodey and Dave.

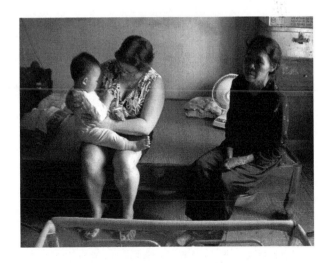

Brodey and I

The rest of the day for us was filled with lots of pictures, lunch, speaking with the caregivers through an interpreter, and waiting for the Justice Department to arrive so we could all sign the final papers and officially be new parents. During the day we all went into the town to buy things that were needed in the orphanage, and we brought the head caretaker with us. We were told that the cradle Brodey slept in used to be lined on each side with mesh, but because he is so big and strong, he destroyed it. Dave and I felt compelled to buy a new cradle for the orphanage. We were pleasantly surprised that the prices were also very low here so we bought two new cradles, an Exersaucer seat, diapers, wipes and whatever else the caretaker said they needed. Some of the other couples bought a bicycle for the women to get to town, they also needed a rice cooker that they were able to get. We had a chance to tour the new facility. It was not too far down the road from the existing one, and it was on a big plot of land, which would be good for the older kids in the orphanage. The baby building was very nice. It was clean and beautiful, Mr. Dao was so proud to show off his new window screens.

When we got back to the orphanage the Justice Department was there and ready for all of us to sign the papers and finally be officially handed our babies. This was all so very emotional for both the caretakers and parents, but it was nothing compared to when it came time for us to leave the orphanage. I knew this would be difficult for everyone involved. We said our goodbyes and boarded the bus. All the caregivers were outside the bus crying, and we were all in the bus crying. Ba, ran back inside the baby house, and came back, climbing onto the bus to give us a blanket. I felt bad, as I know they have limited supplies, but I think for her it was important that Brodey had something from her. While she was on the bus she was wiping her tears and his drool with a little handkerchief, which she also insisted we take with us. I knew this would be hard, but it was agonizing to watch her. When she finally had to leave the bus she stood outside and placed her hand on the window, and I put Brodey's hand up to hers. It was so emotional for everyone. As much as I wanted him in my arms, I knew her heart would be so heavy as her arms would be empty tonight.

Ba and Brodey saying one last goodbye.

As the bus finally started to move, she had to back away. I pray for her every day, thanking God for the love she had for Brodey and hoping she knows the extent of all of our love for him. I send pictures and a letter every year, knowing how much she cherishes them, so she can watch his progress and see how much he is loved.

The next two weeks in Hanoi flew by. It was time to go home. We had the opportunity to leave a few days earlier than expected so we jumped at the chance. My family was having a big party that day, and if we played this right, we would be getting home just in time to surprise everyone. It was a very long travel time with a twelve hour layover in Thailand where Brodey enchanted all the girls in the airport, but we finally made it home. The first place we stopped was my mom's. No one had any idea we were coming so when Erin opened the door when we rang the bell, she burst into tears and couldn't speak. I think she was so relieved that we were home safely, I don't think it registered right away that we had a baby in our arms, she jumped at us then my mom came running out. We headed to my sister's party, when we arrived, everyone was so overjoyed to see us and to meet Brodey. It was a very happy time for everyone.

From the first time we met him, we loved him. He has grown into the funniest, smartest, most talented child, who captivates everyone he meets. He lights up our lives every day. We would like someday to travel back to Vietnam and be able to show Brodey where he was born and also visit the orphanage so they can see what a beautiful, wonderful boy he has become. When people meet Brodey for the first time they always comment on his eyes. Many have used the word "soulful" when describing them. I couldn't agree more; if the eyes are a window to the soul, then I would say Brodey shares a part of his soul with everyone he meets. I have the privilege of seeing those eyes and that little face every day, and it makes me complete.

I feel like the line from an old movie, "You complete me," cliché, I know, but that is how I feel. I can now look at books, or on the computer, or on the street and see those faces and not feel so bereft. How blessed I feel to have been given this gift. People often say to me what a lucky little boy he is that I "found it in my heart" to adopt him. I usually respond that I am the lucky one, he was always part of my heart, we just needed a little help finding each other.

9

"The day we received all of your information and pictures of you, was one of the best days of my life! As soon as I saw your little face, I knew you were the one who has been in my heart all my life."

Journal entry 11/10/07

LEANNE

FOR YEARS I had been interested in psychic mediums. It was not hard for me to believe in these things. I'd had so many dreams of people in my life who had passed where I felt like they were right there with me, or have dreamt of someone in my life that needed me, phoned them the next day, only to have them say, "Oh my gosh, I can't believe you called me. I have needed to talk to someone so badly, and thought of you." For years I had read books about mediums, but being a Christian, was always told I should not believe in "Messengers of the Devil", that it was wrong and these people were somehow evil. However, the more I read, the more I learned that mediums were *helping* people, not hurting them. They were bringing some who had no beliefs to the possibility of finding a spirituality and the Lord.

Wanting to see a medium and actually seeing one were two different things. They seemed too expensive, like you'd have to be on a waiting list for months before getting an appointment. People told me that it was all a hoax, that psychics could read expressions and be able to tell you what you wanted to hear. Sometimes I felt I was being judged, people said they were evil and I should never go to one. As I continued to learn more and more about mediums it became abundantly clear that this was a gift given to them by God. I came to believe they could use their gift to help others cope with loss.

At work one day, a friend was talking about the medium she went to see named Leanne. My friend had an amazing experience that completely changed her life. As I listened to her story I realized that Leanne must be for real, and that there were things she told her that no one else knew. I was so intrigued I immediately took down her name and number, I had to have a reading! I called her later that night and made an appointment for four days later. I know what you're thinking, Leanne had four days to look into my life and do research. Well, all she had was my first name. But, really, how many Midges are there in the world? And I guess from my call, she had my cell number too. From the things she told me, though, there would have had to have been a major CIA investigation into my past. Even the CIA doesn't know what I *think* (do they?). Leanne was able to tell me things I had never verbalized to anyone, I'd only thought them and spoken about them to God or people in my life who had passed.

I was excited to see Leanne. From my memories of the session, I will attempt to retell the story of my session. It was three hours and fifteen minutes long and I still think about it almost every day. It literally changed me and the way I live my life.

I will begin, of course, at the beginning. It was six p.m. when I arrived at Leanne's office. I was very nervous, but excited to see what she was going to tell me. I did not feel like I had a *need* to go, I was just very curious about her gift. When she opened the door I was pleasantly surprised to see a young beautiful woman, who was very soft spoken and had a warm aura. Her warmth put me at ease immediately. When I entered the room it was dimly lit. There were lots of candles, two chairs facing each other, and a cross on the wall. Whew! My nerves settled a bit after seeing the cross. Then I asked her, "Are you a Christian?"

"Yes, I am," she explained. "Let me tell you a little bit about how this all began for me," she said. "I grew up being able to see angels and soon discovered they were giving me messages to pass on to others. As my gift grew I was able to see images, not really people but shimmery light. The figures would show me pictures and I could hear things they wanted to say to the living. I am never given information about the future or bad things, just messages of peace and comfort from angels and people in your life who have passed. If something makes sense to you, Midge, please tell me, and if you do not connect with it, please let me know that as well." It seemed pretty simple to me, but since I was still a little skeptical I figured I might just nod so I wouldn't give too much information away.

As we began the session sitting across from one another, Leanne closed her eyes and said a prayer. When she opened her eyes she gasped, "The angel Gabriel is standing behind you, and he is so beautiful." I wanted to look behind me but held off, knowing I could not see him. It gave me a weird feeling, goose bumps went down my arms and I wondered where this was going. "He is telling me that you dream a lot," she continued "and your dreams are very vivid."

I nodded yes.

"The angel is saying, 'You need to trust what you are shown in your dreams.' He is repeating over and over to 'trust your dreams'. He said you have had a dream and you know which one he is speaking about. Trust what you were shown."

At that exact moment I knew which dream it was. I had only ever told my husband Dave about this dream. It was not something I felt comfortable telling others about for fear of being judged. I even debated whether or not to include it in this book. But after praying about it I realized I was given this powerful dream for a reason, to tell others about it. Not to pass it on would be to deny the awesomeness of God.

In the dream, it is very dark and murky, there is nothing around. I am crouched down, afraid and shivering. I do not know where I am or why I am so cold. I begin to sense a warmth and a light. When I look up there is a bright light, it is beautiful and is radiating out from the center. Standing there in the light I see, with His arms stretched out for me, is Jesus. To me, He looks like so many of the pictures I have seen of Him, but it's not only seeing Him, I can *feel* him, His warmth and love, His face so gentle. I went to Him and was immediately wrapped in His arms. When I was there, it was an absolute feeling of warmth, love and tranquility. I felt like a child again in my father's strong arms, I never wanted to leave. I do not remember *hearing* words, the only way I can explain it is, I remember *feeling* Him say, "I am here. This is where you belong, and this is where you will be, in my arms." I woke with a start, I had tears on my face but I could still feel his love around me. I knew without a doubt that He was my home. I was already a believer but felt so blessed to have been given this gift, and knew with certainty when my time came, I would enter those arms again. Wow! I just lay there praying and talking to Him, thanking Him for that comfort.

Since I was a bit of a skeptic, I was blown away with what Leanne was telling me and the feelings they evoked. After that, she said, "There is an angel who walked in and is standing to your left with two people. They do not want to step forward yet or say anything right now, but they may later. There is also a little girl, very shy and reserved seated to your right in a little chair with a doll." I could not think off the top of my head who that would be. "My mom had a sister who passed away at age two," I said. But Leanne replied, "No, it is not her, I don't know the significance of the little girl right now. The spirits want to start by talking about your daughter."

As I was wondering which one of my daughters, Leanne said, "They are giving confirmation by saying the younger daughter, do you understand?"

"Yes."

"Wow, this is a child of God, she is very spiritual. They keep saying she is so close to God. What a beautiful soul, an old soul. But you already knew that, didn't you? They said you saw that in her eyes when she was a baby."

"Very true," I said with a chuckle. Wow, this was bizarre.

"This child is a lot like you, not only in looks, but she wears her heart on her sleeve. She also has an ability like mine, when the time comes and she shows an interest in it, they are saying to support her, she may feel different from others and will need it."

I would like to stop here for a minute and tell you a little bit about my daughter Erin. When Erin was a baby, a man at work asked me how I could be so sure there was a God. I told him that if he were at my house in the quiet of the night, feeding Erin and having her look up at him with those big blue eyes, he would *know* that God is real, you could see Him through her eyes. It was almost as if when she looked at you, she was remembering what heaven was like. There were several times when Erin was very young, she would say things that would stop me where I stood. The first time it happened, Erin was only two years old. We were snuggling and reading before she went to bed. We were both quiet when I said to her that she was so special and I was so glad that God let me be her mommy. She turned and sat up, looked right at me and said, "No, Mommy, God told me it was because *you* are so special." Then she went right back to snuggling and reading her book. I couldn't breathe for a minute. Had He really said this to her?

Erin was always reminding us all that God was there even when we sometimes would forget. One time as I was changing her diaper, she had a very bad rash at the time that hurt immensely when I had to change her. I said I was so sorry because I knew this would be uncomfortable for her, she just looked at me and began to sing, "Nothing is impossible with God." It was as if she was reminding me to lean on Him when I needed to.

There are two other times that stick out in my mind. Erin, Keegan and I were sitting at the table having breakfast and I had the news on. It was 2005 and Erin was four. The underground in London had been bombed. I was so upset. Keegan and Erin asked me what was wrong. I told them that some bad people did some very bad things in London and many people were hurt. I said we should stop and pray for all the families of the people who were hurt and all the workers who were helping them get out of the tunnel to safety. They both agreed, then Erin looked up at me and said, "Mommy, what we really need to do is pray that God will help the bad guys."

Um, ok, this child was so much further on her journey than me. I didn't even think of that, but I agreed and as hard as it was, we all prayed that God would help the bad guys.

When Erin was five, we were redoing her bedroom, she wanted to get posters to decorate her room. When I asked her where she wanted to go to get posters, she said she wanted angels, so we headed to the Christian bookstore near us. As we stood turning the poster display, she found some angel pictures, one of puppies, then she turned the poster rack again, and gasped. There was a small poster of Christ, a light shining from behind Him. Erin could not move, she was overwhelmed. "He is so beautiful, Mommy, this is the one I want." So when Leanne said she was a child of God, so close to Him, I knew right away what she meant. When I was pregnant with Erin, my mom said she would be my gift from God. She was right, to this day, Erin is a blessing to everyone whose life she touches.

"Now they are moving on to a boy child." I was not going to ask which one, there are three of them. I just wanted to see where she went with this. Leanne kind of laughed and said, "There are a lot of people behind you and they are laughing and saying, 'this one is a clone of his father, just like Dad'. Does this make sense to you?"

"Yes, it definitely does."

She had to be speaking of Keegan. This was really blowing my mind and we had only just started. "This child is very stoic, but has a warm heart. They just keep saying how much he is like his Dad, adventurous, inventive, smart and quiet. He is also an old soul. There have been times that he has made you wonder about past lives?" I couldn't believe she was saying this.

Keegan, for as far back as I can remember, had insisted that he was with Abraham Lincoln in 1860. At the age of three he would draw very detailed pictures of Lincoln and ask me, "Don't you remember, Mommy, don't you remember Lincoln, don't you remember 1860?"

Ok, well no. To tell you the truth, I was always interested in WWII and Vietnam, I really didn't know anything at all about the Civil War. So when he asked me at age three about 1860, I asked him what it was that I should remember. He just sighed and said, "The war! You don't remember the war?"

I told him I would read up on it. At the same time, we were driving to see my older son Rich in Virginia, and on the way Keegan kept saying, "Do you think *that* really old house was in the war?"

I would just say I didn't know, and maybe it was. When we got to Rich's school, Keegan told him that Mommy didn't remember 1860 and Lincoln. Rich was kind of baffled, asking, "What is he talking about?" I told him I had no idea, something about Lincoln and being with him in 1860, something about the war. Rich was amazed and asked, "How does he know that?" I had no idea, I had never even talked about the Civil War. Rich confirmed that in 1860, when Lincoln was elected president, some of the first Southern states seceded.

That was the beginning of the Civil War. It was my turn to be amazed. Keegan, then looking very relieved said, "I told you, I can't believe you can't remember that." His obsession with the Civil War remained for years, including many trips to Gettysburg and any other Civil War forts within driving distance. Needless to say, I have learned a lot about the Civil War.

Leanne then went on to say, "He is an amazing little boy who holds a special place in your heart." I could not have agreed more.

"Wow, there are a lot of people here behind you. They are all so happy that you are here and there is so much love for you in this room." Leanne sits back and stops for a moment. "Ok, they are saying something about a baby. Do you have a baby?" I say only yes, because I don't want to say too much or give anything away. "They want to talk about him."

"They are all behind you, motioning to their faces," she says, adding, "his face is very different from yours. There is nothing wrong with him, he is just very different. Does this make sense?"

"Yes."

At this point Leanne sits back and closes her eyes. She then says, "This doesn't make sense to me, so I am going to say exactly what I am hearing. Please let me know if it makes sense to you, is that ok?"

I nodded and motioned for her to go on.

"They are saying that the way this child came into this world, was strictly a vessel for bringing his soul to you. Your souls were always meant to be together, his soul was meant to be with you. Does that make any sense to you?"

Ok, WOW, yes, yes, yes! Not only did it make sense to me, but right when she said that, it was like a bolt of lightning to my chest. My confirmation -- finally -- that what I had always felt to be true, actually was! "Yes, I understand what that means," I say.

She sits back again and a few seconds later she opens her eyes and says, "Oh my goodness I just heard, 'he is adopted.' Now it all makes sense."

Through the tears all I can say is, "Yes."

I collected myself for a few moments, this was all so powerful. Leanne continued.

"Oh, there is another daughter?"

"Yes."

"She is older, and wow, she is a warrior. She will fight to the death if someone or something threatens anyone in her family."

" That would be my Paige."

"This girl is also an old soul."

This is something I would never have said. Paige is such a ball of sunshine. I used to sing "You are my Sunshine" to her all the time, because she lights up the room as soon as she enters it. I guess I always thought of an old soul as being quiet and thoughtful. Paige was not quiet or reserved, she spoke her mind and if you don't agree, tough luck.

"She comes from a long line of warrior women. She is an artist, isn't she?"

"Yes," I say as I chuckle, this is too much, we had just come home from visiting an art school for Paige that past weekend. Leanne told me to look up warrior women from history, women like Joan of Arc. They were fierce fighters but were also artists, that was their outlet. She then said, "The people in the room with us are suggesting that Paige try to come more from a place of love when someone speaks poorly of her family or friends. Tell her to take a second to step back before lashing out at people."

Paige did not always stand up for herself, but say anything about her loved ones and look out! Paige is a fiercely loyal and loving person. She would, I have no doubt, go to war for someone she loves.

Leanne took a minute then and sat back. "Ok, wow, there is another boy?"

I felt bad, so I told her yes there is another boy, but I also told her it was the last child.

"Ok, I am hearing that you are worried about him, but not in the usual teenage ways. I am being shown pressed clothes, like uniforms, all hung neatly, and shined shoes."

"Yes," that makes sense. At this time my oldest son Rich was in a military college, and had gone to a military high school so he was always clean cut with shined shoes.

"Ok," says Leanne gesturing to her right, "one of the people who came in with the angel has stepped forward. Usually I need confirmation, but this is a strong spirit saying, 'I am her Dad, and that is my boy you are talking about'."

"Yes," I say with a laugh. Anyone who ever knew my dad would agree, he was strong in this life, and I guess that carried on to the next.

"For confirmation, so you know it is him, he is showing me your son's hands. He is working with something metal, I think it might be an engine? Ok, forget that, your Dad is saying it is not an engine. Let me sit for a minute." She then opens her eyes and looks kind of strangely at me and asks if it could be a gun in his hands. I tell her yes. "Your Dad wants you to know and to tell your son, that he was right there over his shoulder when he was working with that gun, and he could not have been prouder."

My son Rich at his basic training graduation at
Fort Benning GA.

Oh my goodness, just a few weeks before this, Rich was on his weekend with the National Guard and they had a contest who could take apart and put back together their rifle the fastest. Rich won the first time around, even against the Sergeant. The second time they did it blindfolded and he lost to the Sergeant by a few seconds. Rich only told this story to my husband and I so I had no doubt that my dad was there with him. My dad then said he was with Rich all the time and was so proud of the man he had become. Leanne then asked if there was a recent graduation we attended where my mom, my sisters and I were saying we wish my dad could have been there. I said yes, my son had just graduated from basic training, he was an Honor Guard, and was Guidon at the graduation, which means he was out in front of the troops carrying the flag. "Your dad wants you to know and to tell your mom and Rich that he was there with all of you, and he was overwhelmed with joy."

"Your dad wants to come back to you. He is saying that the little girl to your right that I mentioned when we started, is you."

Um, ok I am not sure I understand this.

"Well, this is a representation of you as a child. He is saying you were such a quiet and gentle child, and he wants to apologize to you for how stern he was in this life. He says he knew he was not the 'warm and fuzzy' type of Dad that you needed growing up, but he begs you to understand that he didn't know how to be." Leanne then said that my dad was saying that he is with my family every day, because he loves the feeling in our home. Even though he may not have been that "warm and fuzzy" type, he *feels* that in our home and is proud of how I have created that. I don't want anyone to get the wrong idea, I never doubted for a minute that both of my parents loved and adored my sisters and I and were very proud of us. My dad just had a hard time expressing his feelings. It made me feel good knowing he is still around and that he is proud of me. Leanne then said "Your dad is laughing and saying 'You have to tell the girls.' Do you understand who the girls are?"

I say yes, my three sisters and my mom.

She said, "He is saying that his job on the other side is to help people come to terms with their feelings and to express them." He then told her the girls will laugh about this. My mom and sisters did have a laugh when I told them that.

My dad then wanted to talk about my mom. He said he is always with her, and that when weird things happen in the house, that it is him and he is with her. He also said he was worried about her. This is when the second person with the angel joined us. Leann said she was getting a Grandmother feeling, but it is not your grandmother. Ok, who was it then?

"She is giving me confirmation now, saying Helen's mother, does that make sense?"

Yes, it did. My Aunt Mary was my grandmother's sister and she had just passed the year before at the age of 93. We were very close and she took over the Grandmother spot for all of us when my nan passed.

"Mary is saying she is worried about Joanie. Who is Joanie?"

I tell Leanne that Joanie is my mom.

"Ok, Mary is holding out a handful of medicines, saying she is worried about Joanie, but the medicine is not for Joanie, it is for Patty."

Leanne asked me if I understood, and if I knew who Patty was. Patty was my mom's sister Pat, the only one *here* who ever called them Joanie and Patty was Old Aunt Mary. My Aunt Pat at this time was diagnosed with lung cancer and was very ill. I knew my aunt was close to passing and I also knew that my mom was having a very difficult time with the thought of letting her go.

"Your Aunt Mary keeps stressing over and over to tell Joanie that when Patty crosses over, she will be immediately surrounded by love, light and warmth. 'We will all be here to greet her.' Please tell Joanie, she will need to hear this."

I did tell my mom all of this, and I think it helped a little bit when the time came.

I chose not to tell my Aunt Pat about all of this right away. I mean, the time never seemed right for me to just blurt out that I had had a conversation with my dead aunt and we talked about you and dying. I was helping my Aunt Pat one night, when she was close to passing, and she said, "Midgie, I feel like I am so close, it is happening so fast, I am so worried about leaving Billy (her husband)." She also told my mom and me that she had been having dreams about Aunt Mary, and she could not stop thinking of her. I looked at my mom and I knew that this was the right time to tell her everything I had heard from Aunt Mary, via Leanne. By the end we were all crying, but Aunt Pat said it gave her such peace knowing that, and I think it helped us as well.

My Mom and my Aunt Pat at the last
family reunion we had together

I want to take a little break from my session with Leanne to tell you a little bit about my Aunt Pat. My Aunt Pat was a beautiful soul inside and out. She lived her life with a fierce devotion to the Lord, her family and anyone who was blessed enough to have called her a friend. My Uncle Bill and she had been in love since the fourth grade. It was a love and passion that is very rare and should be cherished when it is found. She lived every minute until the very end with passion. I feel that it would be a disservice to *not* tell you what I believe was a gift she gave to all of us at the end of her life. When I say she lived her life right to the end, I really do mean it. She was baking cookies for anyone who would come to visit her up until she was bedridden, four days before she passed. Once she was bedridden, we had to give her pain medication, so she was sleeping a lot of the time. When she would wake she would look up and touch my uncle's face and smile this beautiful smile and say, "Oh Billy, I love you so much, you cannot believe how beautiful it is Billy. It is so perfect, so beautiful." She would then drift off again. Several times before she passed she did this, addressing different people who were sitting with her, telling us all how perfect and beautiful it was. I truly believe she was giving us a little glimpse of Heaven. She passed quietly soon after with the love of her life by her side, holding her hand, knowing she had moved on to that perfect place, but, in his heart, not wanting to let her go.

Ok, so back to my session with Leanne.

"There is one more thing your Aunt Mary would like to bring up before she goes. She is asking about the Easter bread. Do you understand this?"

I could not believe Leanne just said Easter bread! Before I left to come here my mom said in jest, "If Nan is there ask her why my Easter bread doesn't come out as good as hers."

I had to laugh.

Leanne said, "There is another woman with Aunt Mary, and they are both laughing and saying that Joanie will have to figure this out on her own."

My Mom laughed out loud when I told her that.

My Nan on the left and my "Old" Aunt Mary,
at a family reunion

The session had been going on for two hours and I could see at this point that Leanne was tired. She said to me then that there was another person here who was not family but would like to come forward. I was so hoping it was John.

"He is showing me a book, he is holding it and looking over it, he is saying educator, overseer, like a boss, but more like a brother."

I pretty much knew at this point that it was John.

"He is saying that on the way over here you asked him to please come through if he could."

Ok, it was definitely John. There was so much I wanted to say to him. The tears started to flow, I could not hold it back. I told Leanne I missed him so much. Leanne asked me what the relationship was between us here. I told her that we were very close but despite rumors, never intimate. She told me he was agreeing and saying that it was not meant to be that type of relationship in this life, that we were both in different places in our lives when we met. Leanne then looked at me and said, "You were soul mates."

I looked at her questioningly, I always thought my husband was my soul mate.

"Don't worry, you can have more than one soul mate and you are one of those rare people who are very blessed to have found more than one in this lifetime. Many times people go through life never connecting with their soul mates. Your friend says that when you think about him you cry."

"Yes, I can't help it, I miss him so much."

"He wants you to be happy when you think about him, it hurts him to see you cry. He said that when you are thinking about him, *know* that he is right there with you."

It made me feel good to know that, but the tears still manage to come at times.

"He is asking me about a dream or dreams you had of him lately." I explained to Leanne that a few months ago I had taken the kids to the beach for a week. While I was there I could not get John out of my mind, I had dreams where I could feel him there, but would wake up crying and not know why, or what he was trying to tell me. When I went to work that next Monday I told a friend of mine who was also close to John about these dreams, together we decided that whatever he wanted me to know would be revealed eventually. I went to my unit to start my day. As I got to the floor and log onto my computer, John's former wife came around the corner. I was so shocked to see her that I didn't know what to say. We did not really get along when John was alive, but we were cordial with each other. She was visibly upset and said that someone she loved was ill. I felt sorry for her and said that if there was anything I could do for her, to let me know. That was it! I told Leanne that I thought that was the reason for the dreams. John wanted me to try to let go of the past and any bad feelings because he knew she would need that compassion from me at this time.

Leanne said, "Yes, he said that was the message, but he is adamantly saying that this was for you, not because she needed it but because you did. This is the person you are and he wanted you to be able to let go of all that, for yourself, not for her."

Wow, I guess when the Angel Gabriel said to trust in my dreams, he meant it.

"Ok, John is showing me your older daughter's hair? Do you understand the meaning in this? He is saying something about her hair being a 'point of contention?'"

"Yes." When my son was born I named him Richard John, there were many people saying that he was named for John, (John himself being one of those people) I don't think they knew that John was also my father's name. So, when my daughter Paige was born with mops of black hair, there were more speculations, (his wife) wondering every time she saw Paige how she got that black hair? My husband at the time had blonde hair and mine was light brown.

"Well, John is saying that it *was* a "bone of contention" with his wife. He is saying now that he loved those kids and he watches over them and is very proud of them. He whispered that he always did wish they were his."

Then she said, "Now he wants to talk about your baby."

It took me a minute to settle myself down and focus on what she had just said.

"He keeps repeating 'the birthday was no fluke.' Do you understand this?"

"Yes, I understand, Brodey was born on John's birthday."

"He is asking me to ask you to say aloud, right now, exactly what went through your mind when you found out the baby's birthday."

"Ok, the first thing I thought and I had told everyone, was that I knew he was aware of and was on this journey with me."

We had often talked about my obsession with Vietnam, and my wanting to adopt from there. I was hesitant to say what else I had thought, but Leanne was adamant that there was something else. The other thing that went through my mind when I heard the baby's birthday, "I truly felt when I heard, that maybe this baby was a little piece of John."

"Bingo!" Leanne said. "He is waving his arms and saying, 'it is some kind of 'cosmic stuff' that is too complex for you to understand, but a piece of my soul was always meant to be with you'. He also said that he will always watch over this child."

Leanne then sat up and said, "Your friend is holding a

large red leather book. He has it open and is saying, 'I can't wait until you are here with me and I can show you all of the times we have been together in the past'."

I think even Leanne was kind of surprised by this.

Leanne said that the people were beginning to fade. She said my dad was on my left side patting my hand, and John was giving me a kiss on the head and saying goodbye. I got goosebumps right then and began to cry, but they were good tears. My heart was so full, I felt like it might burst.

When I got to my car I said a little prayer thanking God for the chance to talk to the people I love, asking Him to bless Leanne for sharing the gift He had given her. I felt so wonderful and even though I went to see Leanne not because I felt like I needed to, but because I was curious and a little skeptical. I realized then, that I *did* need this and not only did I leave as a believer in Leanne's gift, but that the past three hours and fifteen minutes had changed my life forever.

When I was growing up my relationship with my dad was strained. I knew my dad loved me but I was always afraid of his temper. Even if he was yelling at one of my sisters or my mom, I would go to my room and cry. When I left Leanne I really felt like my dad and I had a new beginning, and that now I could welcome him into our home and I understood better why he was the way he was here on Earth.

When I came home from the session, I called my oldest

son Rich. I told him all about it and the part about my dad showing Leanne his hands and saying he was right over his shoulder at that gun competition. I also told him about Pop saying he was at the Army graduation. He was overwhelmed. It was one thing to say "Pop is watching over you," but to have confirmation of that and to know that my dad was aware of all Rich's accomplishments and was so proud of the man he had become, really impacted him. He was very emotional.

The next day I was able to relay to my mom all that Aunt Mary had said to me. It was still very hard for her to lose her sister, and she is still sometimes angry with her for leaving, but I do think it brings her peace to know Aunt Pat is free of pain and surrounded by love. After being totally amazed that Leanne actually said something specifically about "Easter bread," she was miffed that no one was willing, even from the other side, to reveal their secrets to make her bread better!

As for John, I can't say that I never cry when I think about him. I do still miss him and have so much I want to share with him, but now I know that he does know and is here with me. Sometimes, I feel his presence so much; I look around and am a little surprised not to see him there. I do miss the other side of the conversation though. I know also that he will always watch over Brodey, and though Brodey may have a little piece of John in him, he is definitely his own little soul, he moves to the beat of his own drum and we are all just lucky to be able to have him. He makes all our lives so full and complete.

I know I was blessed with receiving an incredible gift in the things Leanne told me, and I wish that for everyone.

The whole gang, a rare photo of all of us together in Ireland 2011.
From left, Rich, Dave, Brodey, me, Erin, Paige and Keegan

EPILOGUE

WHEN I asked you in the beginning of this book, have you ever met someone for the first time and felt a connection, or maybe felt you knew them deep down in your soul? Well, you do. They are a part of you, good or bad they are here to walk the roads in this life with you. I believe we all have soul families, and sometimes we are lucky enough to meet and recognize people from our soul families here on earth. Whether it is for us to learn by them impacting our lives, or us helping or impacting their lives. We are all on this journey together. Always keep an open mind and when you get that feeling you have known someone, or you feel like you have been someplace before, pay attention to it, you probably do know them or have been there.

I wrote this book because so many people ask the question, "Why did you adopt when you already had children, what led you to that?" They are amazed with the answer, and I usually only give them the highlights. This book is about my struggle throughout my life to understand what I always knew. That my soul was already connected to many people and many lands. I have lived and loved before and I am blessed to have been able in this life to find, *and know*, the souls I have loved before. I hope that through this you can also gain an understanding of your own soul, the souls you were meant to be with, and continue to learn and grow with them. It is also my belief and my hope that if you do have an interest in the spiritual that "Religion" doesn't necessarily condone, pray about it. I have learned in my life that Jesus never puts His hand up to me and says "No." I truly believe that He wants us all to keep talking to Him and to listen to Him as He guides us.

ABOUT THE AUTHOR

MIDGE BRAXTON felt from the age of 10, an inexplicable connection to a place called Vietnam, and eventually a desire to adopt a child from there when she met refugees from the war in 1975. Not understanding these feelings but always searching, she continued with a "normal" life until things started to become clear. Read the emotional stories and experiences of her journey, that culminate with an adoption 34 years later and validation of all of those unexplained feelings.

MY SOUL'S JOURNEY

W. Cly | Eldred | Shinglehouse | W Bingham | Knoxville | Millerton | Jackson Summit | Tioga
xford | Millport | Oswayo | Elkburg | Mills | Elmer | Westfield | Cowanesque | Crooked Cr | Rutland
Coryville | Turtlepoint | Coneville | Raymond | Ulysses | Newfield | Sabinsville | Middlebury Cen. | Mansfield | B
ethport | E.Sharport | Port Allegany | Sunderlinville | West Pike | Gaines | Tansonia | Stokesdale | Sylvania
ma boy | Newer | Burtville | Coudersport | Germania | Wellsboro | Covington | Malesburg
Colegrove | Mina Odin | Sweden Valley | Galeton | Pine Cr | Stonyfork | Blossburg | Morris Run | All
Clermont | Forresthouse | P O T T E R | Antrim | Cr | Landrus | Ogdensburg
bira | Gardeau | Austin | Boris | Cross Ford Jc | Pladachton | Leetonia | Babb | Morris | Liberty
Instanle | Sizerville | Costello | Conrad | Oleona | Cedar Run | Oregon Hill | Hoytville | Roaring Branch | Elle
terburn | Emporium | E.Emporium | Logue | Wharton | Cross Fork | Slate Run | English Center | Ralston | Pleas
burg | Beechwood | Cameron | C A M E R O N | Hammersley Fork | Okome | Eodine | Kellyburg | Proctor
Sterling Run | Dents Run | Stratford | Leidy | Renovo | Hyner | Cogan House | Trout Run | L Y C O M I
Bennett | Grantonia | Driftwood | Sinnamahoning | Westport | Caldwell | Waterville | Cogan Sta. | Picture r
Byrndale | Weedville | Keating | Glen Union | Sallasburg | Jersey | Williamsport | Montours
Tyler | Birch | C L I N T O N | Farrandsville | Antes Fort | Dubotown | S. Williamsport
enfield | Pottersdale | Beech | Lock Haven | Flemington | McElhattan | Montgomery | Collomsville | Allenwd
Odessa | Karthaus | Moshannon | Clarence | Beech Creek | Mill Hall | Rauchtown | Elimsport | Watsontow
rfield | Woodland | Snow Shoe | Howard | Salona | Clintondale | Loganton | New Columbia | W. Milton
A R F I E L D | Kylertown | Yarnell | Lamar | Logan | U N I O N
Woodland | Munson | Viaduct | Fleming | Roland | Walker | Rebersburg | Mazeppa | Lewisbu
Wallaceto | Wigton | Bellefonte | Madisonburg | Hartleton | Mifflinburg | Northumbe
shauter | Brisbane | Osceola Mills | Julian | Axemann | E.Millheim | Woodward | New Berlin
azzam | Cartney | Shoutsdale | Port Matilda | Waddle | Pleasant Gap | Spring Mills | Coburn | Penns Cr. | Subb
rona | Smithmill | Sandy Ridge | State College | Lemont | Or. | Troxelville | Penns Cr
Glasgow | Olive | Vail | Benore | Linden Hall | Potters Mills | Middle Creek | Middleburg | Kreamer
ty | Warriors Mark | Pine Grove Mills | Siglerville | Beaver Sprs. | S N Y D E R | Port Trevorton
rustine | Tyrone | Pennsylvania Furnace | Milroy | Wagner | McClure | Melserville
Dynart | Birmingham | Franklinville Cottage | Roedstown | Shindle | McAllisterville | Dimmsville | Dal
Morrell | Saulsburg | Yeagertown | Maitland | E.Salem | Liverpool | Millersbur
Bellwood | Barre Forge | Belleville | Lewistown | J U N I A T A | Millersown
Juniata | Petersburg | Granville | Mifflintown | Thompsontown | Millerstown | R | Y
B L A I R | Allensville | McVeytown | Pleasant | Port Royal | Newport | Buffal
El Dorado | Altoona | Gusett | Huntingdon | Mattawanna | Spruce Hill | Loganta | Halifa
Canocreek | Connells town | Mill Creek | Mexico | Icksbury | Dauphin | D A U
Hollidaysburg | Royer Mines | Grafton | Newton Hamilton | Honey Grove | Loysville | New Bloomfield | Duncannon | Marysville | Ft. H
ring Spr | Martinsburg | Alton | Mapleton Depot | Clara Run | Shermans Dal | HA
Curryville | Entriken | Calvin | Mt. Union | Capelisville | Perulack | Blain | Landisburg | W. Fairview
Queen | Henrietta | Cassville | Shirleysburg | Bixlersville | Sherman Dal | S | Camp Hill
Woodbury | Dudley | Saltillo | Orbisonia | Blairs Mills | Bloserville | Consdogwu | Carlisle | Mechanica
nterprise | Saxton | Three Springs | Dry Run | McCrea | Grason | Williams Cr. | Williams Cr.
airsville | Riddlesburg | Robertsdale | Meadowgap | Newville | C U M B E R L A N D | Lewisberry
Salemville | Hopewell | New Grenada | Roxbury | Dickinson | Mt. Holly | Dillsburg
Imlertown | Fannettsburg | Oakville | Huntsdale | Spss. | Franklintown | Wellsville
Tatesville | New Grenada | Ft. Littleton | Stenger | Green Village | Shippensburg | Pinegrove Furnace | Urtila | Marille
O R D | Wells Tannery | Bustontown | Metal | Scotland | Benderville | Aspers | York Spr
bedford | Everett | Harrisonville | Knobsville | Chambersburg | Arendtsville | Guernsey | E.Berlin
Mille | Steckman | McConnellsburg | F R A N K L I N | Cashtown | Table Rock | Thom
Clearville | Ft. Loudon | New Franklin | A D A M S | Abbott
sburg | Pineridge | Emmaville | Needmore | Felts | Lemasters | Marion | Orrtanna | New Oxford | Edgegrove

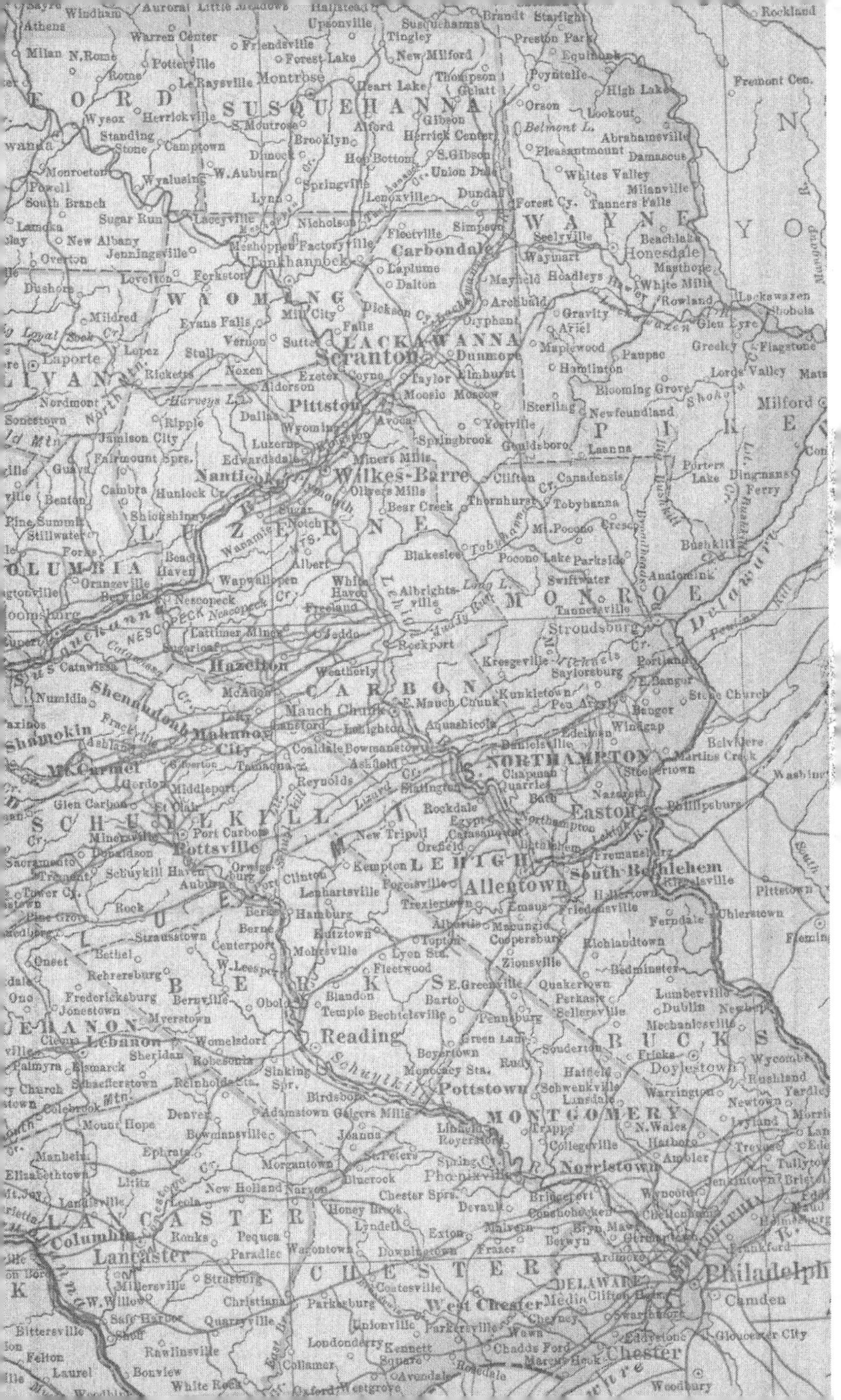

SUSQUEHANNA
WAYNE
WYOMING
LACKAWANNA
LUZERNE
PIKE
MONROE
CARBON
COLUMBIA
NORTHAMPTON
SCHUYLKILL
LEHIGH
BERKS
LEBANON
BUCKS
MONTGOMERY
LANCASTER
CHESTER
DELAWARE
Montrose
Tunkhannock
Scranton
Carbondale
Honesdale
Pittston
Wilkes-Barre
Nanticoke
Hazleton
Stroudsburg
Milford
Mauch Chunk
E. Mauch Chunk
Shamokin
Mt. Carmel
Mahanoy City
Pottsville
Easton
Phillipsburg
Allentown
South Bethlehem
Reading
Lebanon
Pottstown
Norristown
Doylestown
Lancaster
Columbia
West Chester
Chester
Philadelphia
Camden
Gloucester City
Phoenixville
Dunmore
Archbald
Olyphant
Susquehanna
New Milford
Forest City
Laporte
Berwick
Nescopeck
Bloomsburg
Shenandoah
Ashland
Tamaqua
Lansford
Lehighton
Catasauqua
Bangor
Portland
Nazareth
Kutztown
Hamburg
Boyertown
Royersford
Conshohocken
Bryn Mawr
Ardmore
Media
Kennett Square
Coatesville
Downingtown
Ephrata
Lititz
Manheim
Elizabethtown
Millersville
Strasburg
Quarryville
Oxford
Quakertown
Perkasie
Sellersville
Souderton
Lansdale
Ambler
Hatboro
Newtown
Bristol
Jenkintown
Emaus
Coopersburg
Schuylkill Haven
Minersville
Port Carbon
St. Clair
Auburn
Pine Grove
Tremont
Myerstown
Womelsdorf
Robesonia
Sinking Spring
Birdsboro
Spring City
Frankford
Swarthmore
Eddystone
Chadds Ford

Made in the USA
Middletown, DE
10 March 2016